A NEW OWNER'S
GUIDE TO
LOVEBIRDS

JG-703

T.F.H. Publications, Inc.
One TFH Plaza
Third and Union Avenues
Neptune City, NJ 07753

This book has been published with the intent to provide accurate and authoritative information in regard to the subject matter within. While every precaution has been taken in preparation of this book, the publisher and author assume no responsibility for errors or omissions. Neither is any liability assumed for damages resulting from the use of the information herein.

ISBN 0-7938-2853-8

www.tfh.com

A NEW OWNER'S
GUIDE TO
LOVEBIRDS

NIKKI MOUSTAKI

Contents

2003 Edition

In time, you can train your lovebird to perch on your finger.

A pair of lovebirds will keep each other company when you are not home.

There are many different color mutations of lovebirds available to hobbyists.

Lovebirds are intelligent, social birds that make great pets for people of all ages.

The lovebird is a popular pet and is kept by hobbyists all over the world. This is a lutino lovebird and a normal peach-faced lovebird.

INTRODUCTION to the Lovebird

T
he lovebird is one of the most popular members of the parrot family, and has been kept by fanciers and pet owners for more than 400 years. A bird becomes popular for many reasons, and the lovebird embodies most of them: attractiveness, charm, manageable size, easy breeding, variety of color mutations, and much more. Even a novice bird fancier can have success keeping and raising lovebirds—this accounts for much of the lovebird's status as one of the most admired and widely kept companion birds in history.

There are nine species of lovebirds, all in the genus *Agapornis*. Lovebirds are considered parrots—they are members of the family Psittacidae along with all of the other parrot-type birds, called psitticines. Yes, these little birds share characteristics with other parrots, even the macaw.

Lovebirds are originally from Africa and its encompassing islands. Successful-breeding outside of their native lands have made some species as prevalent in captivity as in the wild, perhaps moreso in some cases. Companion lovebirds available on the pet market today don't come from Africa, but from bird breeders, called aviculturists, who rear young birds for sale.

Lovebirds are not imported anymore, so lovebird enthusiasts must rely on captive-breeding stock to breed more lovebirds—fortunately, several lovebird species are easy to breed, allowing the average pet owner to come by this little bird with a minimum of shopping.

As a genus, the lovebird is a stocky, short-bodied bird with a short, square tail. The average size for the lovebird is around 6 inches long, though this varies by 1 or 2 inches depending on the species. The lovebird is among the hookbills family—the beak is curved and shaped much like a hook, rather than being straight and pointed. This allows the lovebird to crack seeds open and to tear apart tough materials, like wood, for nesting.

The wild lovebird flies in fast, short bursts, and is reported to be a pest to farmers, who can't seem to keep this voracious bird out of their crops, especially grain.

Of the nine species of lovebird, each has a distinct region in which it lives, with little overlap. The lovebird's region is primarily temperate, and it does not appreciate colder weather as a result. Although the nine species share many of the same characteristics, they are visually quite dissimilar, and behave differently as pets as well.

The red-faced lovebird was the first of the genus *Agapornis* to be sighted by Europeans, around 1600. In the next 200 years the other eight species were discovered by Europeans, named, brought to zoos, and eventually found their way into the pet trade. Several of the species flourished, becoming widely popular with wealthy Europeans. Eventually, many of the species made it to the US and flourished here as well, making the lovebird a favorite of novices and fanciers alike.

THE NINE SPECIES

There are nine species of lovebirds, though only three of them are readily available for the pet trade. Of those that are readily available there are dozens of color mutations to chose from, making it seem as though there were hundreds of types of lovebirds available. Even though one lovebird might be a vivid green and another a lemony yellow, both birds may be the same species of lovebird. This is to the pet owner's advantage—there is a lot of variety to choose from among the common species. Only a diehard lovebird fancier will keep the rarer lovebird species, which can cost upwards of hundreds of dollars each, whereas even a fancy mutation of a more common species is affordable in comparison.

LOVEBIRD CLASSIFICATION

There are two primary classifications of lovebirds, both of which use visual characteristics to divide the nine species, with an additional intermediate group consisting of two species that don't fit neatly into either grouping, but hold some characteristics of both.

The Eye-Ring Classification

Four species of lovebirds have a noticeable white ring around the eye (called a periophthalmic ring)—these lovebirds are often called the "white-eye-ring group." This group includes the masked lovebird, the Fischer's lovebird, the Nyasa lovebird, and the black-cheeked lovebird.

The Dimorphic Classification

Lovebirds are either dimorphic—having a visible difference between the sexes; or monomorphic—lacking a visible difference between the sexes. There are three species in the dimorphic classification: the Madagascar lovebird, the red-faced lovebird, and the Abyssinian lovebird.

The Intermediate Classification
The remaining lovebirds, the peach-faced and black-collared lovebird, do not fit completely into either grouping. The peach-faced lacks the white eye ring, but shares some of the other characteristics of this group. It is not sexually dimorphic, but an experienced lovebird fancier will often be able to tell the difference between the sexes—there may be very slight variations in appearance between mature males and females.

PEACH-FACED LOVEBIRD
The peach-faced lovebird (*Agapornis roseicollis*) is the most popular companion bird in this genus. Originating in Southwestern Africa, this bird lives in small groups in the wild, and feeds on seeds, berries, and other fruit and plant material. When food is plentiful, a peach-faced flock can number in the hundreds. Closer to home, these birds are readily found in local pet shops and breed prolifically in captivity. This is the species that most people think of when they consider a lovebird. The peach-faced lovebird began its life as a companion bird in the mid 1800s when it was first imported to Europe and successfully bred, though the peach-faced was first discovered (and misclassified) by Europeans around 1793.

Peach-faced lovebirds are about 6 inches long, weighing about 50 to 60

The peach-faced lovebird is the most commonly kept lovebird and comes in a variety of color mutations. This is an orange face peach-faced.

grams. The nominate peach-faced, or, the color most found in the wild, has a bright green to dark green body, an iridescent blue rump, bright reddish face, a horn-colored beak, and black primary feathers. In captivity, the peach-faced comes in a variety of beautiful mutations ranging the whole span of the rainbow, allowing for hundreds of color combinations. The peach-faced is considered monomorphic, though a lovebird fancier, someone extremely familiar with the species, may notice some visible differences between males and females.

A mutation is a color variation that occurs naturally in the wild. Unfortunately, a bird that is an unusual color in the wild is an easy target for predators, and it may not live long enough to pass its genes on to future generations. In captivity, however, bird breeders capitalize on these mutations and breed them into their stock. This is a highly accepted practice and is part of the fun of keeping and breeding the peach-faced lovebird. Mutation is not hybridization, which occurs when a lovebird of one species produces offspring with another species. The resulting birds are considered unfit to breed or show, and some are "mules," birds unable to reproduce. Two lovebirds of different species must never be allowed to breed, though they can be allowed to be lifelong companions.

Hand-fed baby peach-faced lovebirds make remarkable pets, boast enormous personalities, and can be fiercely loyal to their owners. The peach-faced is practically fearless, and will attack birds and other creatures far more sizeable than itself. Some owners say that the lovebird was misnamed—many of these birds have the personality of a tiger!

The peach-faced is not a very noisy bird, in comparison to many companion parrots. It vocalizes in a wonderful light chatter, and will even make a noise like singing or trilling. It makes the most noise just after dawn (or when you uncover the cage) and at dusk. The peach-faced is not a loud bird, but can kick up quite a racket when kept in groups. This bird is reported to be able to mimic human speech, but instances of that are few. Do not expect your peach-faced to talk, though it can learn to whistle and will mimic the calls of other bird species that are housed nearby.

Fischer's Lovebird

The Fischer's lovebird (*Agapornis fischeri*) is found in the wild in Northern Tanzania. This popular bird makes a loyal pet, is a good breeder, and comes in a variety of mutations, though far fewer than the peach-faced. The nominate Fischer's is darker green than the peach-faced, with a bright orange forehead, and olive and yellow on the back of the head and the throat. The beak is a bright red, the rump a violet-blue, and the primary feathers are black. The Fischer's is one of the eye-ring species, meaning that there is a distinctive white ring around the eye. Like the peach-faced, Fischer's are also monomorphic. The nominate Fischer's are readily available in pet shops

A Fischer's lovebird makes a good pet and can be found in several colorations.

or from breeders, and beautiful yellow, blue, lutino, and albino mutations are available for the diligent fancier who is patient enough to look for them. The Fischer's lovebird was named after Doctor G.A. Fischer, who is reported to have made the first sighting of these birds in 1887. The Fischer's lovebird didn't reach Europe until 1926, where they were successfully bred and soon became fashionable pets.

When handled frequently, Fischer's can make good pets, though they can be more aggressive than the peach-faced, and are prone to becoming nippy if left alone too often. The birds in the eye ring group tend to be more independent and aggressive than the peach-faced, though this is not always the case. Like the peach-faced, the Fischer's is not unusually noisy, but can be extremely chatty in groups. It will not talk, though there are very rare exceptions.

MASKED LOVEBIRD

The masked lovebird (*Agapornis personata*) is another popular choice among lovebird fanciers. The masked lovebird originates in Northeastern Tanzania and is commonly found in two colors,

The masked lovebird is an eye ring species and is a favorite among lovebird breeders.

green and blue, both occurring naturally in the wild. The first has a green body, a wide yellow band around the throat, black head and cheeks, a bright red beak, and, like the Fischer's, a white eye ring. The blue version of the masked lovebird has a dark turquoise body, a white band around the throat, a black head and cheeks, and a horn-colored beak. The masked lovebird is also monomorphic. It reached the US and Europe around 1926 and was imported in large numbers, successfully bred, and entered the pet trade a few years later.

The masked lovebird is stunning in appearance, comes in a variety of mutations, and makes a good pet, though, like the Fischer's, must be handled regularly to keep its pet quality. Again, this is an eye ring species, and is often not as amiable at the peach-faced. Like the previous lovebirds, the masked lovebird is not going to bother your neighbors with singing and chatting, though a colony can be quite noisy.

The masked lovebird is a favorite among breeders—these birds thrive in a colony setting and are slightly more of a breeding challenge than the peach-faced. The masked lovebird can be argumentative and needs quite a roomy habitat. It comes in a variety of mutations, though the more rare mutations are not established enough in the companion bird trade to make them readily available to pet shops.

NYASA LOVEBIRD

The Nyasa lovebird (*Agapornis lillianae*), one of the smallest of the lovebird species at about 5 inches long, is uncommon as a companion bird in the US, though some fanciers do keep it for breeding purposes. It is more popular in other countries, such as Australia. This lovebird originates from Northwestern Mozambique, eastern Zambia, and parts of Tanzania and Malwai, though its common name hails from Nyasaland, which formerly comprised many of the countries listed above. Nyasas first came to Europe around 1926 and bred successfully there, though they were misclassified and often bred to other species, such as the peach-faced and the Fischer's.

The Nyasa is in the eye ring group, is monomorphic, and looks a little like a cross between a peach-faced and a Fischer's. It is a lime green with an orangish-red face and head, red beak, green rump, and black primary feathers. There are lutino (yellow) and blue mutations, though they would be difficult to find—indeed, this species is even difficult to find in the nominate color. The Nyasa is said to be the most amiable and least aggressive of the lovebirds, though it is reported to be less resilient than other species. It makes a good pet and breeds well in a colony setting and will accept birds of other species in the colony, whereas the other eye ring species may not.

BLACK-CHEEKED LOVEBIRD

The black-cheeked lovebird (*Agapornis nigrigenis*) is a member

The Nyasa lovebird is the smallest of the nine lovebird species and is uncommon in the US. The Nyasa looks like a cross between a peach-faced and a Fischer's.

The black-cheeked lovebird averages about 6 inches in length. The black-cheeked is a rare find and is not readily available in the hobby.

of the monomorphic white eye ring group, and is one of the larger lovebirds at 6 inches in length. It originates in Zambia and has one of smallest regions of the species. It has a green body and rump, red beak, light orange throat, and a face covered with a black mask. A novice may easily mistake this bird for the masked lovebird, though close study shows differences between the two.

These birds were imported to Europe in the early 1900s and were often bred with the masked lovebird, creating mutations that would have not naturally appeared in the species. Today, the black-cheeked lovebird is among the most rare lovebirds on the market, and it is difficult to find. Breeders no longer cross this species with the masked, but try to maintain the bloodlines. The black-cheeked makes a good pet, but it is so rare (and expensive) that it is best used for breeding purposes at this time.

Madagascar Lovebird

The Madagascar lovebird (*Agapornis cana cana*) is in the dimorphic group and originates on the island of Madagascar, hence its name. This bird is a pest to farmers in its native land, but it is quite prized in aviculture, being far more rare than some of the other species.

The sexes of this bird are easy to tell apart: the male has a grayish-lavender head, throat, and chest, a dark green body, and black primary feathers; the female has no such gray coloring, but a pale green head, throat, and chest and a darker green body, with black

The male Madagascar lovebird has a grayish-lavender head and throat. They tend to be shy and are somewhat difficult to breed.

primaries. The Madagascar is among the smaller lovebirds, at 5 inches or so in length.

The Madagascar lovebird is one of the more skittish lovebirds, though hand-fed babies can be quite tame and make good pets. They are not as easy to breed as some of the more hardy species because of their shyness of people. Breeding of this species began in earnest around the later 1800s, when the Madagascar was imported to Europe. Not many of these birds made it to the US and they are difficult to locate as a result—breeders tended to focus on the lovebirds that were easier to breed, were flashier in color, and had more widely available breeding stock.

RED-FACED LOVEBIRD

The red-faced lovebird (*Agapornis pullaria*) is a member of the dimorphic group, meaning that there is a visible difference between the sexes, though the difference is less dramatic than that of the Madagascar lovebird. It is one of the smaller species, ranging from 5 to 5.5 inches in length. It is characterized by a bright green body

The red-faced lovebird originates in Central Africa and is not commonly found in the US hobby.

and a crimson face. Males have a far redder face while the female's face is more orange and is bordered by a light yellow color. The females beak is more orange than the male's.

The red-faced lovebird is not well known today in the pet community, though it was probably the first lovebird introduced to Europe and bred for the pet trade. It originates in Central Africa and its habitat extends to the west coast. It has the uncanny habit of nesting in termite mounds, a condition difficult to reproduce in captivity, one reason why this species is not as prevalent as some others. It is reported to be a shy bird, and may not make the best hands-on companion as a result.

ABYSSINIAN LOVEBIRD

The Abyssinian lovebird (*Agapornis taranta*), also known as the black-winged lovebird, is a native of Ethiopia (formerly Abyssinia) and is in the dimorphic group, the males and females having a strikingly different appearance. Both sexes have green bodies, but the male has a bright red "cap" on his head just above his eyes and beak, with a thread of red feathers extending around his eye; the female is all green. Both birds have red beaks, wings edged in black with black primary feathers, and they are the smallest of the genus at 5 inches in length.

Europeans discovered the Abyssinian in the early 1800s, though it was not introduced to the pet

An Abyssinian lovebird is also known as the black-winged lovebird. They make delightful pets and are easily obtained through a breeder.

trade until almost the 1900s, when it made its way to Germany and the Britain, and later to the US.

The Abyssinian lovebird is said to make a wonderful pet, though it is not as cuddly as some of the other species commonly kept as companion animals. The Abyssinian is not readily found in the pet trade, though it is a hardy breeder and is kept and raised primarily by fanciers.

BLACK-COLLARED LOVEBIRD

The most rare of the lovebirds, the black-collared lovebird (*Agapornis swinderniana swinderniana*) or, Swindern's lovebird, is not readily available to the pet trade, nor is it even widely available to breeders. This bird was imported to Europe as late as the mid to later 1900s and even so, failed to thrive.

It is a member of the intermediate group, which means it doesn't have an eye ring, nor is it dimorphic. The males and females look alike. This is the only lovebird with a black beak, making it markedly different in appearance from the rest of the genus. It has a green body with olive green around the face and chest, and a noticeable black collar around the nape of its neck. Its rump is blue and its eyes are a pale green or yellow, unlike the eyes of the other birds in the genus, which are primarily black (in the nominate color).

The black-collared lovebird originates in western and central Africa, and their primary diet consists of the figs native to their area, which is one reason why this species does not succeed in captivity.

CHARACTERISTICS of a Lovebird

T he word *irresistible* is a good description for the feisty, beautiful lovebird. Imagine living with a clown, a beauty queen, a loyal friend, and an alligator wrestler all rolled into a 6-inch, energy-packed acrobat. The lovebird is a companion that seems to have it all. Its size makes it a perfect pet for those people living in an apartment, and it lives well in a colony setting for those who have more room to spare. The lovebird can be an ideal pet for someone who wants a close, hands-on companion, or for the person who simply likes to watch birds at play.

WHAT TO EXPECT WHEN LIVING WITH A LOVEBIRD

A lovebird has its advantages over other pets: it doesn't need a litter box or daily walks, it doesn't claw the sofa or bark in the middle of the night, and it doesn't go belly-up when you do a water change or when the electricity goes out. But a lovebird has quirks of its own: despite its name, it can be fierce. It can cuddle with you one moment and bite your finger the next. It needs daily attention and requires an observant owner. This chapter will offer you some factors to consider before you decide that a lovebird is the right pet for you.

Even though pairs of lovebirds can be extremely affectionate to each other, they have been known to squabble and bicker. The term "lovebird" can be rather misleading.

Personality

The lovebird was not aptly named, and the term "lovebird" can be misleading. Its name comes from the observation that two lovebirds will sit closely to one another, preening and cuddling, as if in love. Anyone who owns a bonded pair of lovebirds will tell you that they are loyal and extremely affectionate toward one another, but that they also bicker and squabble, just like human couples do. Though the lovebird can be exceptionally friendly, it can be ferocious and vicious as well, often to the shock of a new owner.

A hand-fed baby lovebird is a cuddlebug, wanting nothing more than to sit inside the collar of your shirt all day and watch the world go by. As it gets older, it will continue to remain affectionate, though it might acquire some surprising habits. For example, a female lovebird may become extremely territorial of her cage and snap at the fingers of her owner, even when the owner is simply trying to feed her. A lovebird may become "angry" with a particular repeated action of his owner. For example, I have a peach-faced lovebird that becomes enraged when I blow my nose. She goes after the tissue with the intent to kill and she doesn't realize that my nose is in it! If I toss a tissue across the room she'll run after it and tear it to shreds, all the while shrieking at it as if telling it not to bother fighting back.

The lovebird has a giant personality akin to that of a much larger bird, such as a macaw. Each lovebird has different personality quirks, just as each human has them. Some lovebirds will take readily to strangers, and some will attack someone new. Some will defend their cages and huddle inside even when the cage door is open, while others will bang the door repeatedly to get out. Most lovebirds are absolute clowns, much to the delight of their owners. They will hang upside-down, "fight" with toys, and perform amazing acrobatic feats.

Companionship

When a lovebird loves you, there is no question of its affection. Lovebirds will do anything to be close to the one they love. The human/lovebird bond can be a strong one, lasting the lifetime of the bird with not a moment of hesitancy. Peach-faced lovebirds make especially good companions when they are acquired as hand-fed youngsters. The eye ring species, such as the Fischer's and the Masked, make good companions as well, but may become feistier than the peach-faced when they come into sexual maturity. This is especially true for the females of the species, who will have a strong drive to nest and defend the cage.

The more you play with your lovebird, the sweeter it will be. Lovebirds that get a lot of hands-on attention become fiercely bonded to their human companions and will be loyal pets for as long as the attention is lavished on them. A lovebird that is left alone for too long, even for only two weeks in the case of an eye ring species, may begin to lose its pet

Lovebirds bond closely to their owners and enjoy playing with their human companions.

quality and can become vicious, or at least nippy. This is not a good bird for someone that wants a "sometimes" pet.

The lovebird shows its affection to its human companion by doing a number of seemingly strange behaviors. It will preen its human's eyebrows and eyelashes, and it will try to kiss its human on the mouth (this is not recommended, because the human mouth contains bacteria that isn't good for a lovebird). A male lovebird will often regurgitate to its human as a sign of ultimate affection. The notion of vomiting as affection is ghastly, but it's actually a very charming gesture! An affectionate lovebird will hide in its human's clothes or underneath long hair, and may even fall asleep there. This is a sign that your lovebird is very comfortable with you.

Intelligence

The lovebird is an intelligent little individual, able to figure out how to escape from its cage or a box, and able to solve puzzles involving a hidden treat or another object it desires. The lovebird, being the high-energy, easily distracted creature that it is, is not the easiest bird to trick-train. Though it could complete tricks and

Lovebirds are intelligent, high-energy birds. Although they can be hand-tamed, they are easily distracted, and therefore not good candidates for trick training.

complicated behaviors with ease, the stubborn lovebird is not apt to follow directions for very long. It would rather do what it wants, than what you want it to do. Take heart, however, that what the lovebird lacks in the ability to learn flashy tricks, it makes up for in loyalty and affection.

Noise Level

A lovebird is not a noisy parrot, but noise is a subjective thing. Lovebirds will rarely annoy neighbors the way a conure or a macaw might, though a lovebird in full chatter can kick up a racket. The more lovebirds you have, the noisier they will be. One lovebird will chirp and call you; two will chirp more and call to one another; more than two and there will be whole conversations going on.

Mess

As with most parrots, lovebirds are messy. Lovebirds provided with a wide dish will inevitably stand right in the middle of it and wildly scratch all of the seeds or pellets out of it and on to the floor. Bathing is a messy affair as well and leads to sprinkled water all over the cage and surrounding area. And then there are the droppings that will manage to find their way into very unlikely places. Female lovebirds are paper-shredding machines and will quickly turn a magazine unfortunate enough to be placed near the cage into confetti. If you are infuriated by mess

Before you decide to get a lovebird, make sure you understand all the responsibilities involved in owning this pet. You will need to provide food, housing, and veterinary checkups for the rest of the bird's life.

or are a die-hard neatnik, a lovebird may not be the pet for you. There are cage accessories and acrylic cages that help to prevent mess, but there's nothing that will eliminate it.

Expenses

Even though you may purchase a lovebird for a reasonable price, it's the cage and the accessories that get you in the wallet. Once you make the initial purchases, however, upkeep of a lovebird (or a pair) is fairly inexpensive. Keep in mind that lovebirds can be highly destructive, and if you don't take precautions, a single lovebird can seriously damage antiques or other expensive items. This is why it's important to "lovebird-proof" your home before your begin living with your new pet.

Here's an idea of the potential cost of keeping one lovebird as a pet.

Lovebird: $25.00 to $200.00 or more
Housing: $65.00 and up
Accessories: $100.00 and up
Feed: $20.00 plus (a month)
Veterinary visit (well-bird checkup): $30.00 and up
Emergency veterinary visit: $50.00 and up

Time Concerns

A lovebird needs a good deal of attention to maintain a certain level of pet quality and emotional health. A lovebird that is ignored may become unhappy and neurotic and may begin to mutilate itself by picking out or chewing on his feathers or other parts of his body. Even lovebirds that live in pairs need your attention. An observant owner who takes the time to notice the behavioral patterns of his or her birds is an owner that can prevent illness and save lives.

It also takes a good bit of time to provide the daily and weekly care that a lovebird needs to remain healthy. Cage and accessory cleaning might add up to four hours or more a week. Cleaning the mess that a lovebird makes takes time, too. There might be times when you will have to cancel a social outing or take a day off of work to hurry your lovebird to the veterinarian in the case of an illness or accident. A person with a heavy work schedule or someone that travels frequently may not have the time required to properly take care of this pet.

Responsibilities

As with any pet, a certain set of responsibilities come with living with a lovebird. These responsibilities should be welcomed—a lovebird provides its owner with more than 12 years of companionship, and an owner should be willing to provide his or her pet with what it needs to live out his life in comfort, health, and happiness.

Here's a list of the many responsibilities that come with lovebird ownership:

- Cleaning the cage daily.
- Giving the cage and the surrounding area a more thorough cleaning once a week
- Offering fresh water at least twice a day.
- Offering and refreshing fruits, vegetables, and safe table foods daily.
- Offering safe playtime out of the cage daily.
- Watching closely for signs of illness and taking your lovebird to the veterinarian if you suspect something is wrong with it or in the event of an accident.
- Lovebird-proofing your home so that it's a safe place for your lovebird to play.

A healthy lovebird can live over 12 years. Will you have the time, motivation, and resources to devote to it?

• Watching other pets closely when your lovebird is out of the cage.

• Checking the cage and toys daily for dangerous wear and tear.

• Making sure your lovebird is neither too warm nor too cold and is housed in a spot that is free of drafts.

YOUR LOVEBIRD'S NEEDS

A lovebird's needs are many, but they are easy to provide. A lovebird needs proper housing and nutrition, time out of the cage and/or room to fly, a safe place to play and things to play with, a companion other than his owner if the lovebird is not a hands-on pet, veterinarian visits (even when well), and an observant, devoted owner—you.

Lovebirds are quirky birds, and have very distinct likes and dislikes. If you were to ask your lovebird his preferences, he would probably answer like this:

"I like room to fly, a lot of time out of my cage, wooden toys, sunshine—but not too much, millet spray, to be scratched on the head (when I'm in the mood for it), paper for chewing, a box to sleep in (even an empty tissue box will do—I'm not picky), fruits and vegetables, music (soft jazz or classical is nice), whistling and having my owner whistle back, scattering my seed all over the floor, shiny objects, bells, bathing in my water dish."

"These are the things I dislike: drafts, cold weather, extreme heat, plastic perches, the veterinarian (though I know I have to go!), loud, sudden noises, being cooped up, being ignored, people who don't know me sticking their fingers or other objects in my cage, fumes of any kind, cats."

LOVEBIRDS AND CHILDREN

Because the lovebird is a small bird and can become snappish, it may not be the right pet for a small child. The lovebird's beak is tough and sharp, and little fingers are very sensitive. The lovebird may be a good pet for an older child, such as one over the age of ten, who is able to understand that the lovebird is an individual with likes and dislikes of its own, and that it may not always want to play when the child wants to.

Children have a short attention span, and they may become disinterested with the lovebird over time. This is a sad state for the lovebird, which will bond closely with the child and will not take

If you allow a child to handle the lovebird, make sure an adult supervises the encounter for everyone's safety.

well to being ignored. Also remember that a child will grow up during the lovebird's lifetime and may move on to bigger things, like college, and may not be able to take the lovebird along. A child that receives a lovebird at ten years of age might have that lovebird until she is an adult of 22 or 24.

Before a lovebird becomes a child's pet, make sure that the child understands the nature of the responsibilities he or she will have to undertake with this creature. Make a daily checklist and post it on the refrigerator or near the lovebird's cage and have the child check off the duties as they are performed. Depending on the child, you will have to make sure that

A lovebird is a pet better suited for older children or adults, rather than small children. Before you give a lovebird as a gift, make sure the owner really wants a lovebird for a pet.

the bird is actually being cared for. When you offer a pet to a child, it's important that you realize that you may have to eventually become the sole caretaker of the pet.

Lovebirds are only good gifts for children (or anyone, for that matter) when it is a lovebird that the recipient desires. No child asking repeatedly for a puppy wants to receive a lovebird, and the child may become resentful of this replacement pet and take out that resentment on the bird. If you really want to give a child a pet as a gift, buy a gift certificate to your local pet shop and let your child choose his or her own pet, with limitations, of course. You could end up taking home a fish rather than a lovebird, but at least your child will have gotten the animal he or she wanted, rather than being forced to care for an unwanted pet.

If you're going to give a lovebird as a gift, try not to bring the animal into the home when there's a lot of hustle and bustle, such as on a birthday or major gift-giving holiday. The bird will be confused and frightened by all of the commotion and may be neglected while the festivities are going on. Again, this is a better time to give a gift certificate or give a photo of the gift bird and pick it up from the store when the holiday is over.

LOVEBIRDS AND OTHER PETS

Lovebirds have a tendency not to get along with other pets. This a huge consideration in the case of people who have many other animals in the house. Lovebirds can pose a danger to other birds in the home if they are allowed to mingle. Lovebirds are territorial and fearless and can injure a much larger bird. A fierce bird of another species may harm the lovebird, who may not realize that it is outsized for the fight. There are exceptions to this rule, however, so you will have to judge the character of your particular birds. However, lovebirds will fight to the death (among themselves and other birds) in a small space, so beware of confining them.

Lovebirds can fall prey to just about any other pet you may own. A dog or cat is deadly for the little lovebird, which will be seen as prey or a toy by these other animals. One little scratch during "play" is enough to kill a lovebird. Ferrets and pet rats will hunt your lovebird, and a fish tank or bowl poses a drowning threat if your lovebird is allowed to wander free in your home.

If you have other pets, make sure that they either get along well, as in the case of other birds, or that they do not have the chance to "get together," in the case of dogs and cats. Never, ever think that it's "cute" to introduce your lovebird to a predator—this is just asking for trouble. A fully flighted lovebird (one without its wings clipped) will be better able to keep itself away from predators in your home, though a lovebird that has full flight can run into other dangers.

LOVEBIRD MYTHS DEBUNKED

The major myth about lovebird ownership is that they have to live in pairs in order to survive. This is not the case. If you have a single lovebird and you act as its friend and companion, it will be

There are several myths surrounding lovebirds. One falsehood is that they must live in pairs in order to survive. A single lovebird can live a happy life when bonded to its human owner. This is a well-adjusted Fischer's lovebird.

Make a solid commitment to care for the birds you choose for your pets.

content and will not need another of its kind. A single lovebird that does not have a human as a close companion should have another lovebird for a friend. A single lovebird will not drop dead from being alone, but it will not be happy either and may eventually become ill or simply pine for company.

Many people think that just because they are small, lovebirds cannot get lonely or anxious. This is a fallacy. Lovebirds need as much attention and care as any other bird. A lonely or mistreated lovebird can develop illnesses and self-mutilating behaviors, which can be deadly.

If you do take on a lovebird as a pet, think ahead to what you're going to be doing in your life. Are there going to be any major life changes? Will you be able to care for this bird in the long term? A lovebird can live 12 to 25 years with the proper care. What will you be doing 12 years from now? Make a solid commitment to your bird that you will care for it for the duration of his life. If you can't commit to a close relationship with a single lovebird, it is best to buy a pair. They will keep one another company, and all you'll have to do is provide the proper diet and housing and maintain an acceptable level of cleanliness in the cage.

CHOOSING the Perfect Lovebird

Choosing the perfect lovebird might seem easy—just visit your local pet shop and choose the prettiest one. That's one way of doing it, certainly, but it's not the best, most informed way to choose a pet that could potentially be a member of your family for more than 12 years. If you've already bought a lovebird on impulse, don't worry—this chapter will help you find it a friend.

WHICH LOVEBIRD IS RIGHT FOR YOU?

Not all lovebirds will have the characteristics you might be seeking in a companion animal. Begin by making a list of all of the factors that you'd wish for in a pet bird. For example, some people will want a very affectionate, hands-on pet; another person might look for a pair of birds to watch and care for; and still another wants compatible aviary birds. Do you want to have to train your lovebird to be friendly, or do you want one that will cuddle with you the first day you own it? Do you want a pair that will eventually breed? The following are some factors to consider.

Species

Of the nine species of lovebirds, only three are readily available in the pet trade: the peach-faced, the Fischer's, and the masked lovebirds. Most of the others are unavailable due to rarity, expense, or poor pet quality. You can, of course, find these other species, but it's more likely that your local pet shop will only carry the most common three species.

Of the three readily available species, the peach-faced makes the most amiable pet. Some will argue this point, but in my experience the peach-faced lovebirds are the most affectionate and least aggressive species of the group. The Fischer's and the masked do make wonderful pets, but they are feisty and can become quite nippy if not handled every day. I am personally very fond of Fischer's lovebirds, but I do know them to be territorial and aggressive, though they are also clever and affectionate, especially if their owners are diligent about hands-on playtime.

Color

If you've decided on a peach-faced, you're in luck—there are

The masked lovebird is one of the three species of lovebirds regularly found in the hobby. Research the different types of lovebirds and choose the one best suited for you.

Peach-faced lovebirds come in a wide array of color mutations. These birds are Cinnamon Slate and Cinnamon Blue.

dozens of colors to choose from. These different colors, called mutations, are naturally occurring in the lovebird, though the primary color in the wild is green. A wild lovebird that is any color other than green would have a difficult time camouflaging itself and may become an easy target for a predator. This is why you won't find yellow or blue peach-faced lovebirds in the wild; they may not live long enough to reproduce. In captivity, however, lovebird breeders capitalize on these mutations and raise baby lovebirds in many different hues.

No one color is superior to another, though it is thought that a bird of the wild green color is a bit hardier than some of the mutations. This may be because many of the mutations, especially newer mutations, are often inbred. The Fischer's and the masked come in a few mutations as well, though these are not as easily found in pet shops as are the peach-faced mutations.

Some of the peach-faced mutations, such as pied or lutino (yellow), are so common that their price is comparable to the nominate green color, while some other, newer mutations are far more pricey. You might find a rather "dull" looking lovebird priced much higher than a "prettier" bird; this is because lovebird fanciers prize the different mutations and because a "dull" looking lovebird can lend its genes to a mate to produce stunning babies of various colors. If you intend to breed your lovebird, you may want to invest in the rarer mutations, which you will be able to find at bird shows or through serious lovebird breeders.

Hand-raised or Parent-raised?

A hand-raised lovebird, that is, one that has been taken out of the nest when it was young and hand-fed by a human, makes a far better hands-on pet than a parent-raised lovebird does. Lovebirds are known to be extremely feisty and self-directed. They do what they want to do when they want to do it. A hand-raised lovebird may actually want to play with you all the time, while a lovebird that was raised by its parents will not see a human owner as a playmate, and will shy from human contact. A hand-fed baby lovebird that is closely bonded with his owner will bang the cage door up and down and do a little "open the cage" dance whenever the owner enters the room. This is a bird that desires close contact with his owner. Parent-raised birds are often said to make better parents themselves and are supposed to be hardier than their hand-fed counterparts, though this is not always the case.

Most responsible pet shops and breeders will not sell you a baby lovebird that is still eating baby bird formula. It's not a good idea for you to try to feed your baby lovebird by hand. If you are

A hand-raised lovebird will be tamer than a parent-raised bird. Ask to handle the lovebird to determine how it was raised and to get a feel for its temperament.

inexperienced with hand-feeding, you can burn, asphyxiate, or cause infection and death in your baby bird. It is better to leave the hand-feeding to someone who knows how to do it. Your lovebird will not be any less bonded to you when fed by someone else. You're the one who will care for it on a daily basis. Your lovebird will come to see you as a friend if you handle it regularly with gentleness and affection. Hand-feeding socializes a baby lovebird to enjoy contact with humans. Often, the hand-feeder will take the time to play with and hold the babies, thus making them very tame and sweet.

You can tell if a group of lovebirds have been hand-fed by handling them. If they don't bite, are tame and calm, and rest easily in your cupped hand, it's likely that someone socialized them to enjoy human contact. A lovebird that flies away from you in panic might not make the best pet.

Age

If you want a very affectionate pet, it is best to buy a lovebird at about eight to nine weeks of age, just after it has been weaned off of baby formula and is eating on its own. You can tell a baby peach-faced lovebird by the dark markings on its beak. These black markings will go away as the baby gets older. A young peach-faced will also have a light rose-colored face area that will brighten around nine to ten months of age or after the first molt.

An older lovebird can make a wonderful pet if it has been handled regularly and is tame and sweet. Unfortunately, most pet shops do not take the time to handle their lovebird stock, so the birds often "revert" as they grow older and lose the ability to be handled easily, becoming skittish, nippy, or just plain vicious. You can tell that a lovebird is mature when it is in full color. A very young lovebird does not have the bright colors around the face that an adult has, though that depends largely on the mutation.

"Recycled" Lovebirds

Many animal shelters and bird rescue organizations regularly have lovebirds up for adoption. Because this is a feisty bird with a reputation for aggressiveness, many lovebirds find themselves out of a home. You may want to put yourself on a list at your local animal shelter in case they get a lovebird in for adoption. Remember that this bird might come with some quirks and may need extra patience and love in order to thrive in his new home. Change is difficult on a bird, so be aware that an adopted lovebird might be anxious until it gets adjusted.

Male or Female?

In the world of lovebirds, especially in the most popular three species, it's the male of the species that tends to be sweet and amiable, and the female that has a territorial, ferocious streak. Males make super pets and are less likely to become nippy. Females are full of personality and spunk, but once they come into full sexual maturity, around 15 months to 2 years of age, they may defend the cage and try to nest in a corner or in a food dish. This can be stressful for the pet owner, but it's not a tragedy. The owner simply needs to continue lavishing attention on the pet and remove any eggs the single female lays. Keeping newspaper and other "nesting" material away from a female lovebird will also help her to remain sweet. A mature lovebird hen who is allowed to shred paper tends to go full swing into nesting behavior and can become aggressive. Because the peach-faced, Fischer's, and masked lovebirds are monomorphic, you will not be able to tell what sex bird you are buying. It really doesn't matter, however, as both sexes make great pets for the owner

You cannot discern between the male and female of the Fischer's, masked, and peach-faced lovebirds. Either sex makes a great pet, although the males tend to be less feisty.

Lovebirds are social and friendly birds. If you have room for an aviary, you may want to obtain a small colony of lovebirds.

who takes the time to play with her lovebird on a daily basis. Even a lovebird hen that breeds can become a pet again in the off-season when there's no nest box to defend.

Number of Birds

Most newcomers to lovebirds are tempted to purchase a pair of lovebirds as pets, thinking that the birds need to be with one another to survive. This is a common myth. Lovebirds certainly do enjoy one another's company, but they don't die if kept alone. A single lovebird makes a far better hands-on pet than lovebirds kept in a pair. In the case of a single lovebird, you act as its "mate," providing the love and affection it needs to be happy. If you don't want a lovebird to be a close companion, consider buying a pair because they are indeed much happier together. Keeping one lovebird alone in a cage with no human or bird contact is cruel. If it happens that your pet is not getting the attention you once provided due to a lifestyle change, consider getting it a friend.

Lovebirds make wonderful aviary birds, provided there is enough space in the cage and there are no other species of birds living with them. Lovebirds are tremendously territorial and will bother and even injure or kill birds far larger than themselves. In a lovebird aviary, give each bird at least two cubic feet of space as a minimum. Do not crowd lovebirds because they can become quite vicious to one another. Females are especially territorial and will kill a newcomer, especially another female, so be sure to establish all the birds in your aviary from the beginning.

If your aviary is large enough, you may add male/female pairs or single males, but be wary of adding single females to an established group. You can mix species in an aviary but do not encourage breeding if you do so. This can lead to hybridization (the mating of two different species), which clouds bloodlines and results in babies that can neither be bred nor shown. The offspring of the peach-faced lovebird and an eye-ringed lovebird are often "mules." They are unable to breed and tend to be aggressive.

WHERE TO ACQUIRE YOUR LOVEBIRD

For many people, a lovebird is often an impulse buy from a pet shop or a purchase made from the heart. Sometimes buyer's remorse sets in once the owner learns of all the details involved with caring for a bird, and occasionally the bird gets aggressive and bites or becomes ill and dies due to a purchase made at a non-reputable store. Buying the right lovebird, one that's healthy and properly

If you buy your lovebird from a pet store or bird shop, take your time to survey the surroundings. The birds should appear healthy and lively. These are good examples of Fischer's lovebirds.

socialized to humans, is easy once you've found a shop or a breeder that cares for their young birds correctly.

Pet Shops

Most pet shops carry a variety of birds along with their other animals. However, the store employees may not have a vast knowledge of birds and may not know much more about a particular bird than the price. The staff at a large general pet shop may not be able to recognize the signs and symptoms of illness in a bird, will know little about the history of a particular bird, and will not have spent much time playing with the birds in their care. If you buy your lovebird from a general pet shop, the responsibility might be on you to choose the best bird of the bunch, though some larger stores do employ staff to deal exclusively with their bird stock.

If you sense that the employees are knowledgeable about birds, the birds seem well cared for, the cages are clean, and all of the birds have fresh food and water, then it may be safe to make the purchase there. Pet shops that keep their birds in unclean conditions or locked away in tiny cages are more likely to sell you an ill bird that has not been properly socialized, or which has lost its pet quality. In this case, buyer beware.

A shop that sells only birds and bird supplies might be a better place to find your lovebird. The staff in the bird shop deals only with birds and troubleshoots bird problems with customers all day long. They are trained to know how an ill bird behaves and may know something about the history and personality of your particular bird. Often, bird shops are willing to provide a new owner with a health guarantee and require a visit to the veterinarian to make the guarantee complete.

It is heartbreaking to purchase a lovebird only to have it die in the first few weeks of ownership. This is why a visit to the veterinarian soon after the purchase is so important—it will show that the place of purchase is responsible for any illness the lovebird may have brought home with it. Always ask for a health guarantee before buying a bird, and get it in writing before you leave the store.

Breeders

Perhaps the best place to buy a lovebird is from a lovebird breeder, one who is involved in the lovebird fancy, and someone dedicated to the species and knowledgeable about the care and

A healthy lovebird will have bright eyes, look alert, and have all of its feathers in good condition. Closely examine all the lovebirds you are considering adopting before you make your final choice. This is a healthy orange face peach-faced lovebird.

training of these birds. Lovebirds are not difficult to breed, so you can often find a reputable breeder by looking in the classified ads in the newspaper, in the back of a bird magazine, or by going to a bird show or exposition. A lovebird breeder is more likely to have the fancier mutations and might be willing to help mentor you through the trials of lovebird ownership. This is someone who cares about the lives of their baby lovebirds and will be available to answer any questions you might have about raising your new feathered friend.

Bird Rescuers

A bird rescue organization is a great place to go if you want to give a home to a lovebird that has been given up for adoption. Sadly, most birds typically only live in a home for two years before they are shuffled along to the next place, and, as a result, there are plenty of homeless birds needing a family to call their own. Do an Internet search on "rescue birds" or call your local shelter to have your name put on an adoption list.

How to Choose a Healthy Lovebird

A healthy lovebird is busy and energetic, bright and attentive, active, and presents a good attitude. A healthy lovebird sings and chirps, has bright eyes, clear nares (nostrils), a clean vent, and is free of debris on its feathers. The feathers should be tight and shiny and cover the entire bird, with no patches missing. The bird's feet should be clean and intact, and the bird should eat with gusto. A healthy lovebird clambers around the cage, hops from perch to perch, and seems lively in general. When it sleeps, it usually does so standing on one leg. Choose a lovebird that has these qualities.

A lovebird that is not feeling well may be fluffed up and sitting on the cage floor in a corner, and look depressed. It may have a discharge from its eyes or nares and a messy vent. The feathers might be dirty from lack of grooming, and the bird may even have patches of feathers missing. It may look sleepy and droopy and keep puffing its feathers to hold in its body heat. The other lovebirds might be picking on this bird because they suspect that something is wrong with it. This is not a lovebird you want to take home, even out of pity. Let the store manager know that you believe something is wrong with this bird.

Overall, it's not a good idea to buy other birds from the same store if you suspect that they're selling an ill bird. Many avian diseases are airborne and need no direct contact to be passed from bird to bird. However, do not overlook a bird that is simply unhappy or being picked on. This bird may just be miserable in its present circumstance and may have feathers missing because the others are plucking them out. Watch the cage dynamics closely to determine if this bird is ill or simply not suited for the hard life of a bird waiting in a pet shop for a good home.

THE FIRST FEW DAYS AT HOME

When you first bring your lovebird home, you will want to give it a few pressure-free days to adjust to the new environment. This

Give your lovebird time to adjust to its new home. It may be nervous and wary of you at first.

Every lovebird has its own personality. After a few days, you can start learning your bird's likes and dislikes, and bond with your new pet. This is a beautiful white-faced blue peach-faced lovebird.

is not the time to begin heavy training sessions or long playtimes away from the cage. Change is difficult for a bird, a creature that likes routine. Think of your lovebird's life before you decided to take it home: it was bred and hand-fed in one place, sold to another place, and now is moving to a third location. That's a lot of adjustment for a little bird!

The first thing you should do is set up your new friend's cage and locate it in a permanent place. This way you won't be adding toys and cups while your lovebird is trying to relax. Once you've placed your lovebird in his new cage and have given it fresh food and water, leave it alone for a few hours so that it can get used to its new situation and scenery. Offer millet spray at this time. It's a good sign of adjustment when your lovebird begins to eat and make noise. If it's cowering and hiding behind toys, trying to be invisible, it may need more time to adjust. Be patient—it will come around eventually. Don't think that your new bird is boring just because it's scared. You would be scared too.

After a day or so, you can begin taking your lovebird out of the cage for playtime. If the bird is a baby, gently scoop it off the perch or side of the cage. Make sure you don't pull hard on its feet, which will be clutching tightly to whatever it's standing on. The baby doesn't know to step on to your finger and you will have to teach it this command. Don't expect too much from your lovebird at first. You're both getting used to each other.

Each lovebird has a different personality and different favorite things. You will learn all about your new bird as the days go on. In this initial stage, move calmly around the bird and play with it very gently. This is the time to build the relationship between both of you, and also the time when your bird will learn to trust you and see you as a friend. If you force an interaction at this fragile time, you may only succeed in scaring your bird, and it will remember you as someone to be feared.

If you play with your bird every day for the first few weeks, perhaps even fielding a few uncomfortable nips with composure, you'll find that your lovebird will develop a sparkling, feisty personality and that the two of you will become fast friends. The change from baby bird to adolescent happens rapidly, and at about four to five months of age a lovebird begins to show how fun it can be.

HOUSING Your Lovebird

O nce you've decided on the type of lovebird you're going to add to your family, you have to consider proper housing. There are many housing options available at your local pet shop, but not all of them are acceptable choices. A lovebird may look like a docile little parrot, but given a few days in his new home, this mischievous little bird will show his new owners his talent as an escape artist, master chewer, and marvelous mess-maker. Proper housing can mean the difference between a safe, happy lovebird and one that's bound for injury—or worse. Providing your lovebird with the right kind of housing and accessories is a major way to ensure its well-being and comfort.

Many people don't like the idea of keeping a bird in a cage because birds are supposed to be free, right? Yes, that's true, but the home offers many dangers for your curious lovebird. A cage will keep your bird safe and out of mischief when you're away. Supervised out-of-cage time is a necessary part of your lovebird's life, but an unsupervised lovebird might get in harm's way—and fast!

Lovebirds housed in the proper kind of cage with the appropriate accessories often love their cages and think of them as Home Sweet Home. A cage is not meant to be a prison, but a safe space for your bird to reside while you're unable to supervise him.

IMPROPER HOUSING: BUYER BEWARE

To begin a discussion of proper cages, let's first take a look at improper cages. Bamboo or wooden cages made to house finches and canaries are attractive but unacceptable for the voracious lovebird, which will make toothpicks out of a wooden cage faster than you can say "Houdini." Cages shaped like pagodas are often too tall and narrow for the lovebird, which likes a lot of horizontal space to clamber around in. Cages with more vertical space than horizontal space are wasted on the lovebird.

Tiny, ornate, showy cages are inappropriate as well. Elaborate scrollwork on a cage can catch little toes or leg bands, causing serious injury. Cages with bars painted or covered with plastic or other materials are a terrible choice for the lovebird, which

46

will spend most of the day picking the material off of the bars. This material can be toxic and can cause death if ingested.

Cage bars should be spaced such that your lovebird will not be able to poke his head through them. If he gets his head through the bars, he might not be able to get his head out again, (much like a child with its head stuck in a banister). A lovebird with its head stuck will panic, which can lead to a broken neck or strangulation.

These are just a few of the inappropriate housing choices available at your local pet shop. Just because a cage is for sale in the pet shop doesn't mean that it's safe or proper housing for your pet.

Finding the Right Cage

Now that you have a list of things to avoid when shopping for housing, let's take a look at housing that will keep your lovebird safe and happy. The right kind of cage isn't hard to find if you know what you're looking for. Any pet shop should carry appropriate housing for your lovebird, but you may have pick through the selection to find what you want. Don't allow the pet store staff to push you into buying something you feel is inappropriate for your pet.

Providing your lovebird with a safe, appropriately sized cage is one way to make sure your bird is happy and comfortable.

There are many housing options available for your lovebird. Be sure to choose a cage that is the proper size to house your birds comfortably.

Proper Size

Wild lovebirds spend most of their days winging around the scrublands, nesting, and foraging for food, and that's a lot of activity for these little parrots. A companion lovebird lives a far different life, but his energy level can surely compete with his wild cousins'. Your pet lovebird may seem like he has "ants in the pants," always moving, always singing and flapping his wings. Lovebirds are animals on the go.

Because of their high-energy level, lovebirds need a large space in which to spend their days. Unfortunately, most store-bought cages are tiny and don't allow the lovebird to expend this energy, which can be turned upon itself in the form of self-mutilation. Most pet store personnel don't know much about birds, and the person helping you may suggest a "parakeet-size" cage, which, frankly, isn't much good for a parakeet or a lovebird. A cage labeled for a cockatiel might be a better choice. If the cage looks like it would generously house several cockatiels, then that might be the one to purchase. Remember, when it comes to cages, bigger is better.

A lovebird forced to spend his days housed in a confined space will be extremely unhappy. Birds are creatures of boundless space, and even though your lovebird was raised in captivity, his instincts tell him that being confined is unnatural. If your lovebird is going to spend a good portion of the day housed in a cage, be sure that you buy the largest that your space and budget can afford. The minimum length for a lovebird cage should be at least 3 feet (36 inches), though the width and height can vary from 18 inches to as large as you want. Your bird should be able to actually fly from perch to perch. This means that it should take wing-power to get from one side of the cage to the other. Most "lovebird-size" cages only allow a wing-assisted hop, or force the bird to clamber on the bars to move around. This size cage is too small.

Proper Shape

The perfect shape for a lovebird cage is a large square or a large, long rectangle. Corners in a cage will make a lovebird feel comfortable and give it a tight space to crawl into when he's feeling insecure or sleepy. A round cage might be attractive but offers far less security than a square cage, and, unless it is very large, offers far less room to fly.

The bars on the lovebird's cage should be primarily horizontal, with a few vertical bars for structural purposes. Horizontal bars allow the lovebird to climb around its cage and hang safely on the side.

Proper Materials

The proper material for a lovebird cage is uncoated steel or wrought iron. Other metals may contain harmful toxins, and a coating on the cage bars is a tempting "treat" for the lovebird, which may ingest this harmful material and become ill or die. Many cages come in a combination of metal and plastic, which is fine for the lovebird. Acrylic cages are a nice choice for the lovebird because the solid walls prevent mess, though they don't allow for climbing and can be quite pricey.

Safe Doors

Commercially made cages commonly come with three types of doors. The best types of doors for the lovebird are the doors that open downward (like an oven door) or to the side (like your front door). Doors that slide up and down (like a guillotine) are the most common type, but can cause your bird serious injury. Lovebirds are extremely good escape artists and can quickly learn how to open this

Lovebirds are good escape artists and can teach themselves how to open their cage doors. Be sure that your cage door is securely latched at all times.

door, but some lovebirds may not be able to open the door well enough and it will come slamming down on his neck. If your cage does have this style of door, consider buying spring clips or another type of lock so that your bird can't slide the door up.

The Cage Bottom

The proper cage for a lovebird is one that has a grating or a grill on the bottom so that the lovebird is prevented from rolling around in his own mess. Lovebirds are notorious for shredding paper and for tossing things in their water, and there's nothing a lovebird would like more than to be able to get to the material on the cage bottom and play there. This is exceptionally unsanitary and can lead to serious illness. In the wild, lovebirds are never exposed to their own fecal materials the way they are in a caged environment. You should take care that your lovebird is exposed to as little of its own waste material as possible, and a grate on the bottom of the cage will help this.

PLACING THE CAGE

Now that you've decided on a cage, you have to consider where in your home your lovebird is going to live. This is an important decision that can make the difference between a very happy bird and a miserable one. Try to look at this from your lovebird's perspective. It might be convenient for you to house your bird in the garage, but is the bird going to get enough attention, light, fresh air, and warmth there?

Your lovebird's cage is best placed in a location that gets a lot of traffic, like the family room, living room, or the room where everyone watches television. A place where there's too much swift-moving traffic, like a hallway, isn't a great location, however. The cage should be in an area where there's a sense of relative calm, but is well-attended by the members of the family.

Because your lovebird needs a good deal of attention, an out-of-the-way location isn't the best choice because he will begin to miss his "flock" (you and your family) immediately if relegated to a back room. The garage is too drafty and is prone to fumes. The

Your lovebird's cage should be in an active, but not overly noisy area of your home. The lovebird will enjoy the chance to socialize with you throughout the day.

bathroom and kitchen are both places that are prone to wide temperature ranges and chemicals, neither of which are healthy for a lovebird. A child's room might be dark and quiet for most of the day while the child is at school, and too noisy at other times. Again, the family room is your best bet.

Once you've decided on the room where your lovebird is going to live, choose a corner location for the cage and try to make sure that the cage is covered on at least two sides by the walls, because this will make your lovebird feel safe. A cage that's standing or hanging in the middle of the room will make for an extremely insecure bird. When the family cat appears, or a car backfires outside, your lovebird will want to retreat to the back of the cage. A cage that's freestanding will have no "back" and no place for the lovebird to "hide."

To make your lovebird feel even more secure, especially if you can't place the cage next to a wall, you can surround the cage with safe, nontoxic plants. Be aware that a lovebird will make quick work of a plant and chew it to bits, so you should carefully supervise your bird when he is out of the cage.

The corner where the cage is set up should be free of drafts. Lovebirds can tolerate cooler temperatures, down to 50 degrees Fahrenheit for short periods of time, but they dislike wind, no matter how slight. Lovebirds can't bear extreme heat either, so make sure that the location of the cage maintains a reliable, warm temperature.

Don't place the cage directly in front of a window, even though this seems like the thing to do. Lovebirds are extremely alert creatures and will become alarmed by predators lurking outside. These predators can take the form of the neighbor's cat or dog, hawks circling in the sky, rats and raccoons, and even cars going by. (Imagine having to be on guard all the time!) The sun shining in a window may overheat your bird if he can't get out of the sunlight. It's okay for your lovebird to be placed *near* a window, but not directly in front of it, unless the cage is so large that part of it extends over onto a wall.

Placing a commercial cage outside on a patio or porch is extremely risky. It will leave your lovebird very vulnerable to predators outside, and a cage is no match for a determined raccoon or opossum. A thief might also be tempted to steal your lovebird, cage and all. Furthermore, the pet lovebird housed on a patio might not get as much attention as it would housed in a family room. Some people choose to house multiple lovebirds in large cages on an enclosed patio or porch, which is fine, because in this case the lovebirds have each other for company and the cage is far too large for a thief to take. A cage on a patio should be double-wired, that is, two layers of wire placed one over the other such that a predator would not be able to reach the feet of the birds inside. A rat or raccoon can actually pull a small bird through the wires of a cage. If you live in a place that gets very hot or very cold, you might want to consider housing your lovebird inside.

Cage Accessories

Now that you have bought the proper cage and found the perfect location in your home for your lovebird to live, you have to furnish

Offer your lovebird a variety of different sized perches made of different materials, such as wood and concrete. This is a peach-faced, its young age is indicated by the dark marks on its beak which will disappear as it gets older.

the cage with all of the necessities and goodies that your lovebird will need to be happy and healthy. You might be surprised at how many items you will have to buy, but many of these are one-time purchases and should last the lifetime of your bird.

Perches

Most commercial cages come with a couple of smooth, wooden dowels to use as perches. These are fine to use, but they are an inadequate selection for a lovebird, which spends most of its life on its feet.

A wide variety of perches can help to maintain your lovebird's foot health. A lovebird that stands on the same perch day after day may develop foot sores, lameness, or other foot disorders. These are easily remedied by offering various perches made of assorted materials in many different dimensions. Your lovebird should have perches that make him stand with his feet widely spread out (almost flat) and perches that allow his toes to almost touch one another when he's gripping them. Fortunately, there are many different types of perches on the market, and they are easily found at your local pet store.

Wooden: Perches made of wood are the standard choice. However, the smooth wooden dowels that come with a commercial cage don't offer much footing for your lovebird. You can remedy this by scoring them every half-inch or so with a razor blade. This will give them more texture and they will be easier to grip. Manzanita wood and choya wood perches are nice in that they offer a natural look and feel and come in many different dimensions. Wood is also great for chewing. Don't be angry at your lovebird when he chews his wooden perches to bits because this just means that he appreciates them! You can use "green" wood from trimmed trees from your backyard as perches, but you must first make sure that the tree is nontoxic and that it has not been sprayed with fertilizer or pesticides. Lovebirds will enjoy chewing the bark and leaves off of citrus branches, for example.

Concrete: Concrete perches are a necessity for your lovebird, which will use them to keep his nails and beak trim. Offer two concrete perches of different dimensions, but be sure that these aren't the only perches you offer because they can irritate the feet. Lovebirds will often choose a concrete perch to sleep on because it offers good footing. A concrete perch might also be used as a "napkin" after a particularly messy meal, so be sure to clean them regularly.

The sandpaper sheathes that slip over perches are not the same as concrete perches, and, in fact, are prone to causing foot problems. The sandpaper is very abrasive and can cause sores, and the paper tends to get wet and hold bacteria in it. This is not something you want under your lovebird's feet.

Rope: Rope perches are fun to play with and come in a variety of dimensions and colors. They can be twisted into all kinds of shapes to fit in your lovebird's cage. Your lovebird will have a ball shredding the rope, but you must make sure to check it every few days for loose strands that can wrap around a leg or neck and cause serious injury. Keep all ragged stands neatly trimmed.

Plastic: Plastic perches are easy to clean and inexpensive, but they are not pleasant to stand on. Use a minimal amount of plastic perches and make sure that you provide other types of perches as well. Some acrylic perches come with toys attached, and these are a nice addition to the many perches you will offer.

Cups

The standard commercial cage usually comes with two square, plastic cups designed to fit neatly into doors located toward the bottom of the cage. These cups are fine to use, but they are by no means the best choice for your lovebird. Plastic cups are difficult to clean, not only because the square shape does not allow thorough cleaning of the crevices, but because the plastic eventually becomes scratched and bacteria will grow in the scratches. A standard cage usually has places for the cups at the lower half of the cage, which might allow waste to fall into the cups. Plastic cups also tend to break and they are lightweight enough for a busy lovebird to turn over and dump the contents.

Replace plastic cups with three pairs of round, stainless steel cups. This means that you will have six cups: two for water, two for seed/pellets, and two for fresh foods. Use only one set at a time, and allow the other set to be thoroughly washed and dried before its next use. Stainless steel is easy to clean and is very durable. Ceramic cups are breakable and will eventually scratch. Many stainless steel or ceramic cups come with no-dump holders, so you won't have to worry about spillage. Lovebirds are notorious for scattering seed and spraying water, so you might want to consider a hooded cup that will help prevent mess.

Some people use water bottles or self-watering tubes to dispense water. These often become clogged or dirty, and owners tend to refresh the water less frequently. A coop cup filled with clean water at least twice a day should do nicely.

TOYS

Toys are a must for the high-energy lovebird. A lovebird without toys to fling, chew, snuggle, and argue with will be a bored and unhappy lovebird, indeed! The single lovebird must have many toys to play with. A pair or colony of lovebirds will still enjoy playing with toys, but it is not necessarily essential for them to have as many. Toys give your lovebird something to do while you're away and offer much-needed exercise to a cage-bound bird.

Safety first is the motto when it comes to toys for your lovebird. Beware of toys that are flimsy or have small spaces where a toe can catch. Your lovebird's head should never be able to fit in a ring that comes on a toy. Toys that are made for much larger or smaller birds should never be considered. Toys labeled for cockatiels and conures are usually appropriate.

There are a vast assortment of perches, toys, and other cage accessories available at your local bird shop. Only choose items that are safe for lovebirds.

Spend time examining and handling the lovebird you wish to purchase.

Soft, wooden toys, often combined with leather, hard treats, and lava rocks are a great choice for the lovebird, which will enjoy chewing the wood. Make certain that all colored wood is made with natural dye. The toy should indicate the type of dye on its label.

Tough acrylic toys are great, but plastic toys made for parakeets are not a good choice because your lovebird has a powerful beak and can break these easily. Toys with bells will be especially appreciated, but make sure that the clapper is firmly attached or it might get swallowed. Jingle-type bells are not appropriate for lovebirds because the birds may get a beak or toe caught in the small opening and become seriously injured as a result.

Preening toys that contain rope, sisal, feathers, or floss are fun, especially for the single lovebird, which will enjoy having something to preen other than itself. Be careful, however, with fraying rope toys and make sure that you keep all loose strands trimmed.

Lovebirds absolutely adore swings, so make sure that you provide your pet with at least one. Some swings come with toys or beads attached, which add extra things for your lovebird to do. Mirror toys are good for a single bird, but if you notice your lovebird becoming too attached to his reflection, you might want to take that toy away and replace it with something else. If not, your lovebird might prefer its "mirror mate" to you.

Homemade toys are great when used with supervision. Toilet paper rolls cut into rings and hung on sisal rope are very entertaining, as is a shallow ceramic dish containing marbles, popcorn, and dry cereal.

Rotating your lovebird's toys is a great way to keep them "new" and allows you time to clean them. Buy more toys than will fit in the cage at any one time and rotate them in and out of the cage on a weekly basis. Don't remove your lovebird's absolute favorite toy, however, as this can cause undue stress.

OTHER ACCESSORIES

Now that you've taken care of the essential cage accessories, here's a list of other indispensable items that your lovebird will need to thrive.

Bird lamp: If you live in a northern location that is dark for much of the year or if your lovebird lives in a room that doesn't get much light, you should invest in a bird lamp. There are many available on the market, or you can simply buy a spotlight from a hardware store and equip it with a bird or reptile bulb from your local pet store. This high-spectrum bulb provides your lovebird with the "natural" light it needs to maintain his health. A bird kept without the proper light can become malnourished. You can keep the light on for nine to ten hours a day.

Cage cover: Your lovebird does not need his cage covered at night, though people that like to sleep a little later in the morning might do well to invest in a dark cage cover. A cover also serves to keep out drafts and to quiet noisy birds during the day. Don't use the cover for extended periods of time in daylight hours. It should only be used for a few minutes to calm raucous birds in the event that you need them to be silent. Be careful that the cover does not become frayed. If the cover is very thick, the extreme darkness in the cage may frighten a lovebird. If you hear flapping or distress in the cage when you cover it at night, flip up a corner of the cover and let some light through.

Nightlight: If your bird becomes frightened at night or if you have a cat roaming the house, you will want to keep a nightlight on in your bird room. This will give your lovebird a sense of security. It will be able to tell the difference between a real predator and someone making a midnight snack in the kitchen.

Cage locks: Most lovebirds are quite proficient at escaping from the cage. Invest in spring clips or another type of lock and keep them on the doors at all times. Twist ties work well too, but the metal inside the tie can be dangerous if your lovebird frays the paper surrounding it.

Mineral block and cuttlebone: These items provide much needed calcium to your lovebird's diet and are fun to chew and destroy. Make sure that your bird has at least one of each, and replace them when they become soiled.

Millet holder: Lovebirds will do anything for a millet spray, and a special holder will keep the spray attached to the side of the cage and not on the cage floor, where it can become soiled.

Birdy kabob: A birdy kabob is a metal stick on to which you thread all kinds of goodies, such as fresh fruits and vegetables. The stick is usually capped on the end with a plastic ball so that there's no sharp point. The kabob mimics eating behavior in the wild and makes your lovebird exert some energy to get his food.

Flooring: Your lovebird's cage should have a metal grating on the bottom so that he can't get to his mess, but you will need to put something in the bottom of the cage nonetheless. Regular newspaper is the easiest choice, and if you change it at least every other day, it's sanitary as well. Many people use corncob or other types of litter for the cage bottom, but these tend to hold moisture and might be cleaned less frequently because they often don't look dirty when they are.

Bird Bath: Your lovebird will want to bathe, and will do so in its water dish unless you provide it with a special bath. There's no stopping your bird from bathing in the water dish, but a larger, shallow bath offered several times a week might help.

Playgym: A playgym is like a little exercise stand for birds. Your lovebird might appreciate a cage-top playgym, complete with ladders, toys, and even a cup for snacks. But don't be surprised, however, if your curious lovebird becomes bored with the playgym and moves on to something more fun, like your curtains.

Seed catchers: Lovebirds are messy creatures and are always searching for that "perfect" seed, which is inevitably at the bottom of the dish, making it necessary to toss all of the other seeds out on to the floor. A cage bloomer or plastic seed guard will go a long way to keeping the seed inside the cage.

Mite protectors: You will find mite protectors for sale in your local pet shop. There is no need for this item, and, in fact, the chemicals inside can be harmful for your bird. Instead of the mite

Be sure to provide your lovebird with cage accessories such as toys, a mineral block, a birdbath, and a millet holder. These items will improve the quality of your bird's life and keep him from getting bored in the cage.

protector, take your bird to the veterinarian for a checkup. It's unlikely that your lovebird has mites, or that it will contract them.

SETTING UP THE CAGE

You now have what seems like far more cage accessories than a little bird needs. Take heart, however, that your lovebird will use and appreciate all of these essential items provided they are set up properly in his cage. Here's a cage setup checklist to help you place everything appropriately.

1. Make sure that all of the parts of the cage are put together correctly and securely.

2. Place full food and water cups toward the front of the cage and about midway to the top. If the doors where the cups should go are too low, don't use them. Use a cup holder instead.

3. Place perches at various levels toward the middle to the top of the cage, making sure that there are no perches above food or water dishes. Lovebirds prefer to be at a high point in the cage, so don't position perches too low. If you place perches above one another they are going to become soiled.

4. Place the millet holder, cuttlebone, and mineral block on the sides of the cage near a perch. Don't place these items too low where they can be soiled.

5. Place toys in various spots around the cage, making sure that they don't block the food and water dishes.

6. Pull out the tray and add newspaper to the bottom of the cage below the grate.

7. Add bird (or birds).

8. Place the spring clips or locks on the doors.

You're done! Your lovebird is home!

CLEANING YOUR LOVEBIRD'S CAGE

When you have lovebirds, expect to do a good deal of cleaning. Not only do lovebirds soil their cage, but they will also make your floor look like a farmer has just sown a crop there. The smart lovebird owner invests in a good handheld vacuum.

Daily cleaning chores include changing the paper in the bottom of the cage (you can do this every other day if you're pressed for time), soaking the dishes (you should have two sets) in a ten percent bleach solution, and making sure there are no waste deposits on the perches.

If you want to keep several lovebirds and have room, you can build an aviary for your feathered friends. Be sure the aviary is safe and secure from the elements and potential predators.

Weekly chores include disassembling the cage (if it's small enough) and cleaning it thoroughly with a bleach solution or kitchen soap and a scrub brush, scrubbing all the perches, and cleaning and rotating toys. A larger cage can be hosed down outside.

Many household detergents and cleansers are extremely dangerous for your lovebird. You can use vinegar as a disinfectant and baking soda as a cleanser (don't mix the two, however). A ten percent bleach solution is fine as well, as bleach is nontoxic to birds. Of course, make sure you rinse everything thoroughly before putting your lovebird back in the newly cleaned cage.

CAGE ALTERNATIVES

Because lovebirds appreciate being together—at least, they do when they have enough space—they make excellent colony birds and can be kept together in large aviaries or habitats. An aviary is a large cage where birds live and a habitat is a large aviary that tries to mimic the birds' natural environment. An aviary allows lovebirds to do what they do best—fly. This is a wonderful gift that you can give your birds, and anyone with any amount of space can have an aviary or habitat.

Lovebirds do not cohabitate well with other bird species, and they will attack birds far larger than themselves, so do not house them with any other kinds of birds. They will even quibble amongst themselves, especially if there's not enough room for each of them. Provide at least two cubic feet per lovebird in an aviary situation.

The Aviary

If you want to create an aviary for your multiple lovebirds, you must first find a spot that's safe, semi-shady, and free from dampness and standing water. Remember, predators will want to eat your lovebirds, so you must double-wire the cage. This means that there will be a layer of wire on all sides about an inch away from cage, as if there's a cage within a cage. This is the only way to keep your lovebirds safe.

Remember, your aviary needs a good, solid roof, and your birds will benefit from an enclosed addition to the aviary where the birds can go to sleep and get away from inclement weather. Lovebirds will not tolerate extreme temperatures, so if you live in a climate that gets very hot or very cold, consider an inside aviary or a greenhouse-type habitat.

If you are going to build your own aviary, make sure that the materials you use are non-toxic, such as untreated wood. Wire from the hardware store is often coated with zinc, which is deadly to birds. Scrub and wash all wire thoroughly before use using a vinegar and water solution, then let the wire spend several weeks outside in the weather.

Once you have your aviary built, add your birds all at once. Adding a newcomer once the colony has been established is often deadly for the new arrival. It's best to add your lovebirds in male/female pairs, with at least three pairs minimum, as this will minimize fighting among the group. Offer several food and water dishes because the dominant female in the group might try to hinder the other members from eating. Make sure there are plenty of perches and things to do in the aviary such as wood to chew, cornhusks to nibble, toys to rattle, and swings to play on.

If you decide to breed your lovebirds in the colony setup, make sure you place the nest boxes as high as they can go and offer several more boxes than there are pairs in the aviary. An established colony should get along peaceably and is a real pleasure to keep.

NUTRITION for Your Lovebird

Lovebirds are not known to be picky eaters, but they do get used to a certain diet readily, and that means that a poor diet can be difficult to change. Feeding your lovebird properly from the very beginning will help keep it in top shape and keep your veterinary bills low. If you look around a pet shop, it might seem that all you have to do is feed your lovebird seeds and change his water, but this diet can actually be compared to feeding a prisoner solely bread and water. Not only is an all-seed diet unhealthy, it will barely sustain a lovebird, much less let it thrive.

There's a lot of emphasis placed on good avian nutrition these days, which can make the effort to feed your lovebird properly a little confusing. There are so many different products on the market such as seed mixes, pellets, supplements, and treats—where should you begin? This chapter shows you a simple way to feed your lovebird properly and how to get the most nutrition out of the foods you offer.

Feeding your lovebird a well-balanced diet is one way to keep your feathered friend in the best of health.

STARTING YOUNG

Your baby lovebird is used to eating a certain diet when it comes into your home. It is important that you maintain this diet because any sudden change in diet can cause your baby bird to stop eating and become fussy. Lovebirds are active, have high metabolisms, and can lose weight drastically if they

Keeping your lovebird on a healthy diet can be a time-consuming task. If you don't have time to prepare fresh foods every day, plan ahead and keep the food in the refrigerator or freezer.

don't eat, and this is a dangerous situation. Instead of making your lovebird go "cold turkey" on a new, better diet, begin offering new foods gradually and show your bird that they are good by nibbling on them yourself. You can't force a lovebird to gorge on something it doesn't recognize as food, such as a leaf of kale, but if you keep offering it day after day, the bird will eventually check out the new item. Some owners become frustrated with their birds because the bird refuses a food item for several days. It can take up to two weeks or more for a bird to begin to nibble at a new food, so if you are determined that your lovebird try carrots, keep offering the carrots every day, even if it seems like a waste of time and carrots.

A Note on Consistency

Some bird owners become very enthusiastic about their bird's diet for the first few months, making sure that it has the proper amount of everything it needs. Eventually this enthusiasm wanes and the bird is once more on an unbalanced diet, which it quickly gets used to eating. It may be difficult to get your lovebird to eat properly again, so you want to make sure that you choose to feed a healthy diet that you can maintain. This might mean preparing foods in advance and keeping them in the freezer, or chopping veggies the night before you feed them, but all of this effort is worth it when you realize that you're doing something essential for the health of your lovebird.

FRESH WATER

Clean, fresh water is essential to your lovebird's well-being. You should offer bottled or filtered water only, and make sure that you refresh it at least twice a day. Lovebirds are notorious for making "poop-soup," and tossing everything into their water for a nice soak. This can cause bacteria to flourish and make your bird ill if it drinks this nasty concoction. Adding a drop or two of apple cider vinegar will help retard the growth of bacteria in the water and is healthful for your bird as well. Supplementing the water with vitamins is not recommended. The vitamins provide bacteria with nutrients for spawning, thus turning your bird's water into a slimy mess. Your lovebird's water dish should be clean enough that you would have no problem drinking from it. You should have two sets of water dishes: one in use, and one soaking in a bleach solution and drying for use the next day. Water bottles tend to become clogged, harbor bacteria in the tube, are more difficult to clean, and owners tend to change the water in them less frequently. Water tubes are also less likely to be changed as often as they should be. Instead, use a stainless steel coop cup for water. Your lovebird may bathe in it and toss his food inside, but that's what lovebirds do. You'll just have to clean it more often. The bonus to that is that your lovebird will always have fresh water.

THE BASIC DIET

Most lovebird keepers feed their birds a diet based on seeds, with the addition of fresh foods. An all-seed diet is deadly for the little lovebird, but a diet that includes seeds can be very balanced if you also offer other, more nutritious items. Seed is fatty and doesn't have all the nutrients that your lovebird needs to remain healthy. A lovebird eating only seed will begin to suffer from various maladies and can eventually die of them. Seed is a fine base diet as long as you complement the seed with other healthy foods. The seed labeled for cockatiels at your pet store is the appropriate mix to feed your lovebird. You can feed a "fancy," expensive mix if you notice that your lovebird enjoys it, but most lovebirds will do fine with a plain

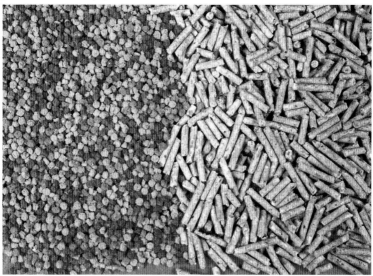

You can offer your lovebird a seed diet, a pelleted diet, or a combination of both for balanced nutrition. Consult your veterinarian if you have questions about what to feed your lovebird.

You can feed your lovebird a variety of fresh fruits and vegetables. Offer your lovebird a sample of different foods to find out which ones he prefers.

seed mix. Remember, seeds are not all you are going to feed your lovebird.

Keep seeds in an airtight container or in the refrigerator or freezer so that they do not become contaminated with seed flies. Use a clean scoop to dole out the seed instead of dipping your bird's contaminated dish into it.

Seed Diet Versus Pelleted Diet

Some manufacturers produce a pelleted diet, which consists of small nuggets into which all of the nutrients your lovebird needs are supposedly compacted. Pelleted diets are relatively new on the scene for parrot-type birds, having been used for poultry for many years. Not much is known about the long-terms effects of birds eating these manufactured diets. Furthermore, a small pellet prepared for a lovebird is also the same pellet prepared for a parakeet, a cockatiel, and a small conure. How can it be that these very dissimilar birds can thrive on the same formula? Their metabolisms are different and their propensities toward obesity and activity are different as well.

Some avian experts recommend the use of these diets, suggesting that the bird need only eat these nuggets and nothing else. For this active, curious lovebird, this is a very boring proposition. Some people feeding pellets as a base diet also include produce and table foods, but this is not recommended according to the pellet manufacturers. This is not to say that you shouldn't feed pellets—

they should be a nutritious, fun addition to your lovebird's diet. Offer them in conjunction with all of the other foods you feed— variety in a bird's diet is the key to good health. Pellets are also a great addition to many bird-specific recipes and add a lot of nourishment to the cooked foods you offer your lovebird.

VEGETABLES AND FRUITS

Vegetables are an important part of your lovebird's diet. Veggies offer a variety of nutrients that your lovebird needs to survive. Although fruits are high in sugar, some are so rich in nutrients that they are worth the calories. Feed produce that is dark green and orange in color as these items are rich in Vitamin A, a nutrient that your lovebird needs for good respiratory health. The following is a list of vegetables and fruits that you can offer every day. Remember, variety is key. Offer as many as you can of these items daily.

Vegetables:
asparagus
beet tops
beets (raw or cooked)
broccoli
brussel sprouts
carrots (raw or cooked)
celery
chard
collard greens
corn
dandelion
endive
green beans
green pepper
jalapenos
kale
mustard greens
pear
peas
pumpkin
red pepper
spinach
watercress

yams (cooked)
yellow pepper
yellow squash
zucchini

Fruits:
apples
apricots
bananas
berries
cantaloupe
cherries
figs
grapefruit
grapes
honey dew
kiwi
mango
oranges
papaya
peaches
pineapple
plums
watermelon

Limit the snacks and treats you offer your bird, otherwise you will spoil his appetite for his regular, more nutritious foods.

Make sure to remove all fruit within a few hours of feeding it, otherwise it may spoil or attract fruit flies. Cooked veggies should also be removed within a few hours if you live in a warm climate.

TABLE FOODS

Your lovebird can eat just about anything that you eat. The healthier table foods that you can get your lovebird to eat the better. With the exception of chocolate, avocado, alcohol, and salty, sugary, and fatty foods, your bird can eat everything on your plate. Share your meals and be persistent if your bird is reluctant to try new foods—keep offering them and your bird's curiosity will get the best of it. It might seem like cannibalism, but your lovebird might even enjoy a bit of turkey or chicken. Don't forget to bring a "birdy bag" home with you when you go out to eat.

SNACKS

The love for our birds is often expressed with treats—seed sticks, seed balls, seed, seed, seed. Too much of a good thing is still too much. Limit seed treats to once a week and treat your lovebird to a special type of fruit or other healthy snack. This will keep your lovebird from gorging on "candy" and keep his appetite fresh for more nutritious foods. Don't give up on treats though; your lovebird may enjoy the occasional sweet seed stick.

Healthy, low-fat snacks include air-popped popcorn, healthy cereal, whole-wheat crackers (spread with peanut butter for the occasional sticky treat), and whole wheat bread.

Favorite Foods

You will find that your lovebird chooses a couple of favorite foods. This is great if those foods are healthy and nutritious. For example, if your lovebird's favorite foods are kale, carrots, and red peppers, you can feel free to feed them every day. If your bird's favorite foods are millet, celery, and watermelon, you might want to begin limiting those foods and offering more nutritious options, but that does not mean that you have to exclude those favorites forever.

DIETARY SUPPLEMENTS

Some lovebird owners add supplements to their birds' diet. Common supplements include cuttlebone, mineral block, and calcium powder. Some people drizzle supplemental oils over their birds' seeds and sprinkle supplement powder on top of that. This

Your lovebird will let you know what his favorite foods are. Make sure you offer your bird nutritious snacks and treats.

Offer your lovebird an occasional treat or snack, but do not overfeed him. Healthy snacks will give your lovebird the nutrients he needs without making him overweight.

Offer your lovebird safe toys to play with. There are several types available in your local bird shop. Rotate the toys so your bird does not become bored with them.

is not harmful for a lovebird, and can even enhance the diet. Consult your veterinarian before you begin to supplement your lovebird's diet. A lovebird that relishes produce, table foods, and pellets, and eats a small amount of seed should not require a supplement, though laying hens may need more calcium during breeding season.

Grit is not recommended for lovebirds. They do not really need it, and they may gorge on it and become very ill and even die as a result.

EXERCISE AND NUTRITION

No discussion of nutrition would be complete without a note on exercise. You know that if you eat a completely healthy diet but do not exercise, you will not immediately become fit and trim. The same goes for your lovebird. If your lovebird is housed in a large cage or aviary and is allowed to fly, you can be assured that it is getting the exercise it needs. Flying is the best form of exercise for a bird. If your lovebird lives in a small cage or has its wings clipped, you should make sure that it gets the exercise it needs to remain healthy and fit. This means playing with your lovebird in an active way. You can place him at the bottom of a rope or bird ladder and have him

Seed is a good base diet for a lovebird, but is by no means a complete diet.

climb up, or have him climb from your hand to your shoulder as a game. Even a clipped lovebird enjoys a good wing-flapping session and will appreciate being out of the cage so that he can flap away without hitting a toy or the bars of the cage.

Recipes

Cooking food for your lovebird is a great way to provide nutritious, safe, and fun foods. Here are a few recipes that you can try. You can freeze portions of each of these and thaw each day for a new, fresh treat. All of these recipes are easy and variable. Feel free to add whatever you happen to have in the kitchen.

Lovebird Bread

Buy a package of corn muffin mix and follow the directions on the package. When you have the batter mixed, add $1/2$ cup pellets, $1/2$ cup dried fruit, $1/2$ cup canned beans (any kind), $1/2$ cup broccoli (or other veggie), 2 tablespoons of crushed cuttlebone, 2 tablespoons chunky peanut butter, and anything else you think your lovebird might like. Bake until a knife comes out clean from the center of the bread. Note: it may take far longer than the package recommends.

Lovebird Pancakes

Make pancake batter the way you normally would (if you're like me, use instant), and add 1 cup pellets, $1/4$ cup dried apricots, and $1/4$ cup shredded carrots. Make like regular pancakes. You can add anything else to the batter you think your lovebird might like.

Lovebird Omelet

Crack several eggs into a bowl (including the shells), and add pellets, two types of chopped veggies, dried fruit, and anything else your lovebird will like. Cook as an omelet or scramble. Cook this extremely well because chicken eggs can pass on disease to parrot-type birds. Freeze, and thaw a small portion each day.

Lovebird Pasta

Boil whole-wheat pasta and drain. Pour it in a saucepan and melt soy cheese over it. Add pellets, veggies, bananas, crushed hardboiled egg (including shell), or whatever else your lovebird likes. You can freeze this in ice cube trays and defrost a cube a day. It makes a nutritious and colorful treat.

HEALTH CARE for Your Lovebird

A well cared-for lovebird can live for 12 to 15 years. However, it's a sad fact that these little birds rarely live beyond five to seven years due to accident or illness, many of which can be easily prevented. This chapter will help you recognize the signs of illness in your lovebird, show you how to create a safe household environment, and give you tips on how to deal with common emergencies.

CHOOSING AN AVIAN VETERINARIAN

An avian veterinarian is a doctor who has been trained to treat the illnesses and injuries of birds. The avian veterinarian has experience with recognizing and treating illnesses particular to birds, whose bodily systems are different from those of a dog or a cat. Your avian veterinarian is your first line of defense in keeping your lovebird healthy. Once you acquire your new lovebird, you should make an appointment within the first three days to see an avian veterinarian near you. This "well-bird" checkup will ensure that your bird is

Be sure to take your new lovebird to the avian veterinarian for a checkup at least once a year. The vet will examine your bird and make sure he is in the best of health.

healthy, and it will begin a relationship with the doctor that will last the lifetime of your bird. Many veterinarians will not treat emergencies unless the patient is already registered at the office, so you might find yourself in a dire situation if you haven't created this valuable relationship.

You should take your lovebird to the avian veterinarian at least once a year. This will enable the doctor to weigh the bird and to do some routine tests, which will show any changes and indicate any potential disorders. This is also a good time to discuss your bird's diet and have the doctor trim your lovebird's nails.

Choosing an avian veterinarian takes a bit more effort than just finding one near your home. You will want to make sure that the doctor has a good bedside manner and is open to your questions and concerns. Ask the veterinarian if she has birds of her own—it's a good sign if she does. Find out what hours the office is open, and what the emergency policy is. You will want to find an avian veterinarian who will speak to you in the middle of the night should your bird become injured.

When you visit the office, look around to make sure that it's clean and talk to the staff to see if they are friendly and efficient. Remember, this is a relationship that will last the lifetime of your bird, so you might as well make it a good one.

Four Easy Steps to a Safe and Healthy Lovebird

Keeping your lovebird healthy is easy with a little effort and know-how. By following these four steps, you can keep your lovebird healthy and safe throughout its lifetime.

Visit an Avian Veterinarian

Keeping your lovebird healthy is easy with a little effort and know-how. First and foremost, a visit with an avian veterinarian will show if your bird is suffering from any ailments or diseases, and will offer your bird early treatment. Often, a bird with a disease that has progressed too far may never truly recover and will have a shortened lifespan as a result of the damage the disease has done to the bird's delicate body, especially if the disease involves the respiratory system.

Feed Your Lovebird a Nutritious Diet

Nutritional deficiencies account for many ailments and can

lower the protective response of the immune system, making a lovebird more susceptible to disease. Ensuring that your lovebird is eating a proper diet will go a long way toward keeping him healthy.

Keep Your Lovebird's Cage Clean

Keeping your lovebird's cage clean and disinfected will help keep disease away. A lovebird living in a filthy cage, drinking dirty water, and eating from a cup soiled with feces is a bird in jeopardy of becoming ill. Clean your bird's cage thoroughly at least once a week and make sure it's dry and free of crevices where mold or fungus can grow. A ten percent bleach solution works well for disinfecting and it is safe for your bird as long as you rinse the cage thoroughly. A solution of vinegar and water is also safe to use as a disinfectant.

Lovebird-proof Your Home

Lovebird-proofing your home and taking precautions so that your lovebird avoids injury is essential to keeping your bird safe. Lovebirds are frequent mischief-makers. If there's something hazardous in your household, your lovebird will be sure to find it. These four simple responsibilities—veterinary care, proper nutrition, cleanliness, and creating a safe environment—are crucial to ensuring a happy, healthy life for your lovebird.

SIGNS AND SYMPTOMS OF AN ILL LOVEBIRD

Lovebirds, like most birds, tend to hide their illnesses until the disease is quite advanced. A wild lovebird that shows itself to be ill is vulnerable to predators, and will try to behave as normally as possible for as long as possible. Your lovebird has the same idea. Knowing what to look for in an ailing lovebird will help you to recognize the illness early, which is key to treatment and speedy recovery. Here are a few symptoms of illness to be on the lookout for.

Excessive sleeping: An ill lovebird may sleep too much, especially during the day. Sleeping on the bottom of the cage is particularly significant.

Fluffed-up appearance: If you notice that your lovebird is fluffy, he may be trying to maintain his body temperature and could be fighting off an illness.

Loss of appetite: You should know how much food and what types of food your lovebird is consuming each day. If you notice

Take all the necessary precautions to keep your lovebird safe and healthy.

that your bird is not eating or is eating far less than usual, he could be ill.

Change in attitude: If your lovebird seems listless and is not behaving in his usual manner, for example, if he has become cranky or limp, call your veterinarian.

Lameness: If your lovebird can't use his feet or hold up his head there's something wrong. Possible reasons include injury and egg-binding. Consult an avian veterinarian immediately.

Panting, labored breathing, or tail bobbing: These symptoms might signify a respiratory illness or overheating.

Discharge: If you notice runniness or discharge on the eyes, nares, or vent, there may be an illness present.

Change in droppings: Your lovebird's droppings should consist of a solid green portion, white urates (overlapping the green portion), and a clear liquid. If the droppings are discolored (very dark green, black, yellow, or red) and there has been no change in diet (such as feeding beets or blueberries), there might be a problem. Also, if there's a pungent odor or the droppings have a more liquid texture than usual, call your veterinarian immediately.

Debris around the face or on feathers: This indicates poor grooming or regurgitation, both of which are potential signs of illness.

Seizures: If your lovebird is flailing in his cage and there are no obvious signs of it being caught in his cage or on a toy, rush the lovebird to your avian veterinarian.

Severe change in feather quality or quantity: If your lovebird begins to lose feathers in patches or you notice him picking them out, call your veterinarian for an appointment.

Quarantine

Quarantine is traditionally a period of 40 days in which a new bird is kept separate from birds already established in the household. Some people choose to shorten this period to 30 days and find no harm in doing so. During the period of quarantine, a new bird is watched for signs of illness. You should feed and water the new bird after you care for your other birds and change your clothing and disinfect your hands after any contact with the bird or its cage. Quarantine is the only way to prevent a new bird from passing a potential illness to the birds you already own. It is sometimes not possible to completely separate a new bird from established birds, but you should try to do your best to keep contact at a minimum while the new bird is being quarantined.

COMMON LOVEBIRD DISEASES AND AILMENTS

Lovebirds are prone to several diseases and ailments, many of which are preventable and treatable by your avian veterinarian. The following section details a few of the most common ailments that lovebirds are known carry or contract. Use this information as a guide only. **Never** try to diagnose or treat your lovebird without consulting your avian veterinarian first. There are treatments

Quarantine a new lovebird for 30 days when you bring him into your home. Watch him closely for signs of sickness to be sure he doesn't pass an illness on to your healthy birds.

available over-the-counter that often make the situation worse for an ill bird. Do not medicate or treat your bird for a suspected illness until you seek the advice of a professional.

Nutritional Disorders

A lovebird on a poor diet will soon begin to suffer from a variety of disorders, including obesity, tumors, foot problems, feather disorders, and a decreased immune system that will leave the bird open to disease. Common symptoms of nutritional disorders include overgrown beak, yeast infections, bulging fatty tumors, lameness, swelling in the feet, and discoloration of the feathers in extreme cases.

To ensure that your lovebird does not suffer from these easily preventable ailments, offer a balanced diet and include, on the advice of your avian veterinarian, nutritional supplements in the

You can have your vet check your birds for parasites such as roundworms and red mites.

recommended doses. Poor nutrition will cut your lovebird's lifespan by more than half of the potential 12 to 15 years.

Parasites

Giardia is a one-celled protozoan that can affect your lovebird, other animals in the house, and yourself. Giardia is passed through tainted food or water and distresses the digestive tract. It can cause diarrhea, itching, the inability to digest foods, and weight loss, among other symptoms. Have your veterinarian test for this problematic parasite that is often resistant to treatment.

Roundworms are sometimes found in the digestive tract of lovebirds and should be tested for on your first veterinary visit. If roundworms are found, routine tests and treatments should be done on the bird. Getting rid of these pesky worms can take quite some time.

The *feather mite* is not very common in lovebirds but can plague birds that live outdoors in filthy conditions. Red mites feed on their host's blood and are highly contagious. If you suspect mites, do not attempt to treat them yourself. See your avian veterinarian for treatment options.

Bacterial Infections

Mycobacterium avium is responsible for the tuberculosis infection in lovebirds and can be transmitted in food, water, or unclean cage conditions. Avian tuberculosis can be transmitted to humans with compromised immune systems, so the caretaker must be careful to avoid infection. Though tuberculosis in humans is a respiratory disease, it is principally a digestive infirmity in lovebirds. Symptoms include weight loss and digestive disorders.

Psitticosis, also called chlamydiosis and Parrot Fever, is also transmittable to humans and causes respiratory distress symptoms in both humans and birds. Psitticosis is transmitted through droppings and other contaminated discharge.

Viral Infections

Psitticine Beak and Feather Disease (PBFD) is an incurable, highly contagious disease that results in feather loss and beak lesions. Diagnosis is through a blood test, and euthanasia is normally suggested with a positive result. This disease is fatal. Symptoms include feather loss, abnormal feather growth, and a generally ill condition.

Polyomavirus typically affects young lovebirds, though adult birds carry the disease and transmit it to their young, who die around the time of fledging. Polyomavirus occurs mainly among

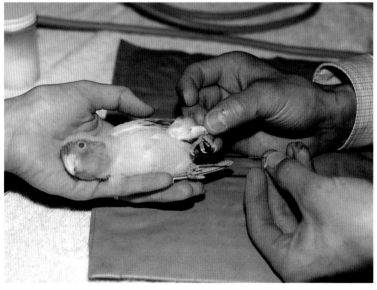

The avian veterinarian will have to take a blood sample to test for viral infections such as polyomavirus that can be harmful to your birds.

breeding birds, though households with many birds are susceptible as well, especially if you are going to be bringing young birds into the household. There is no treatment for polyomavirus at the moment, though there is a vaccine. Have your avian veterinarian test all of your lovebirds for this disease.

Pacheco's disease is a type of viral hepatitis that affects the liver. It is fatal and is primarily diagnosed upon death, which occurs quickly. Pacheco's is a highly contagious disease and can be transmitted easily when acquiring a new bird. Enforce strict quarantine at all times.

Fungal Infections

Yeast infections, or candidasis, affect the mouth and digestive system and can involve the respiratory system as well. Your lovebird generally has a certain amount of yeast in its system already, but when the bird is undernourished or has been through a regimen of antibiotics, the fungus yeast can grow to excess, causing health problems. A lovebird with a yeast infection will have a sticky material in its mouth and may have white mouth lesions. Regurgitation and digestive problems may occur as well. Treatment by a veterinarian is required. Even though this condition is not immediately serious, if left untreated, it can cause death. Offering your lovebird foods rich in vitamin A, such as green leafy vegetables and orange fruits and vegetables, can help prevent yeast infections. Vitamin A supplements may be recommended.

Aspergillosis is a fungal infection that causes respiratory distress and can be deadly for a lovebird. Any changes in your lovebird's breathing and vocalization, or gasping and wheezing can signify this infection. Aspergillosis is diagnosable by your avian veterinarian, but it's difficult to treat, and may take months of medication and treatment. You can prevent this infection by keeping your lovebird's housing and surroundings very clean and dry.

THE MOST SERIOUS HOUSEHOLD DANGERS TO LOVEBIRDS

Though lovebirds can live to be at least 12 years of age, many do not make it due to accidents in the home. The average family home is a minefield for the curious lovebird, which will manage to find its way into things you never imagined, often with deadly consequences. The following are the most common household dangers to the little lovebird.

There can be many dangers present in your household, including other pets, standing water, and even common cleaning products. Keep your bird safely in his cage when you are unable to watch him closely.

Predators

The family dog poses a huge threat to the lovebird, and the family cat is an even deadlier enemy. Dogs of certain breeds may be able to be trained not to go near a bird, but a cat should never be trusted, not for a moment. Dogs such as terriers and sighthounds are dangerous to have around a little bird because their instincts tell them to pounce on small, quick-moving objects. One slight nip from a dog, even in play, can mean death for your lovebird. Cats don't even have to bite to kill a bird because they have a bacterium on their claws and in their mouths that is extremely toxic to birds. If your cat scratches your bird, the bird will die within 48 hours unless immediate treatment by a veterinarian is sought.

Water

Standing water is a strong temptation for a lovebird which may want to take a bath or drink. Unfortunately, the bird may fall into a pool deeper than it can remove itself from. Many lovebirds drown in toilets, large dog bowls, fish tanks and bowls, half-full drinking glasses, ponds and fountains, hot tubs, full sinks (with dishes soaking), and pots of boiling water. Keep your toilet lids down at all times, and keep all exposed water covered, even if you think your lovebird can't get to it.

Nonstick Cookware

Any cookware labeled "nonstick" emits an odorless fume that, when heated, can kill a bird within a matter of moments. It was previously thought that the fumes only occurred when the nonstick surface was overheated, but research now indicates that it is emitted at even low levels of heat. Birds have tremendously sensitive respiratory systems. Remember the canary in the coalmine? Miners took a canary into the mine with them and when the canary died the miners knew there were fumes present and they left the mine immediately. If you notice that your lovebird is in distress and there's no apparent reason, check for gas leaks or other fume-causing agents, such as scented candles, fireplaces, and heated, nonstick surfaces.

Many items other than pots and pans can have nonstick surfaces. These include heat lamps, portable heaters, plates on irons, ironing board covers, stove top burners, drip pans for burners, broiler pans, griddles, cooking utensils, woks, waffle makers, electric skillets, deep fryers, crock pots, popcorn poppers, coffee makers, bread makers, non-stick rolling pins, lollipop molds, stockpots, roasters, pizza pans, and curling irons. Even a well-ventilated room isn't safe when there are nonstick items being used. Toss your nonstick items and get used to cleaning pots and pans with a heavy-duty scrubber! Do not risk killing your bird for convenient cooking.

Common Household Products

Keep all household cleaning items away from your lovebird. These include soaps, drain cleaners, laundry detergents, floor cleansers, and bathroom cleaners, all of which might be a tempting treat for your lovebird—with tragic consequences.

Items commonly kept in a garage should be stored neatly away from your bird. These include fertilizers, pesticides, and barbeque products, such as charcoal and lighter fluid. Realize that your lovebird can easily tear through paper bags.

Items that are regularly sprayed into the air can also cause severe respiratory distress or death. These include air freshener, fabric freshener, and scented candles. Lovebirds will want to munch on candle beads or other waxy items like crayons. Markers, pencils, and pens can also be deadly.

Toxic Houseplants

Lovebirds are chronic nibblers and always seem to be shredding something to bits the moment you turn your back. Houseplants are a serious temptation for lovebirds, which are naturally attracted to them. Even one nibble of a toxic plant can poison your lovebird and cause death. See the appendix for a partial list of toxic and safe houseplants.

Ceiling Fans

Birds have a natural instinct to climb or fly to the highest spot that they can find. A high spot is generally safe from predators and is a good lookout point. A ceiling fan seems like the perfect spot for a fully flighted lovebird. Now, imagine a lovebird flying around a room and a ceiling fan on—it's a deadly image. One good whack from the blade of a ceiling fan is all it takes to bring your lovebird down for good. Make sure all ceiling fans are kept off or have them removed.

Open Windows and Doors

The threat of a fully flighted lovebird flying out of an open door or window is a serious one. Many lovebirds that take flight outdoors are never seen again. Keep all doors and windows securely closed or screened when your lovebird is out of his cage or make sure that its wings are clipped properly. Even if you believe that your lovebird is attached to you and would never leave, a loud noise such as a car backfiring might frighten your lovebird into flight and it may become confused and not find its way back.

Having a lovebird fly away is a heartbreaking experience. If your lovebird flies away there's still hope that the two of you will be reunited—your bird is not necessarily gone for good. First, watch where the bird goes. If your bird is very friendly you may be able to coax him down from a tree or other spot with a treat, such as millet spray. Keeping an eye on your bird until nightfall is the key to a quick recovery. Once it gets dark, your bird will "roost" and you might be able to capture him easily with a bird net.

If your bird lives in a pair or has other bird pals in the house, take the other birds outside in a safe carrier and encourage them to whistle for the lost bird—you can do this by whistling to them. Take your bird's cage outside and fill it with millet spray and tie open the door with a twist tie—your bird might come down at the sight of his cage filled with treats. It's a good idea to make a recording of your

Keep a watchful eye on your bird when you allow him time out of his cage. If he is fully flighted, he may try to escape through an open door or window.

bird's vocalizations—the sound of his own voice may bring your lovebird back home.

If you are unable to pinpoint the location of your lost bird right away, begin making calls to all of your local pet shops, veterinary offices, and shelters, describing your bird and offering a reward for his safe return. Make fliers and posters and hang them in places that get a lot of foot traffic, such as grocery stores. If you don't have a photo of your bird, clip one out of a book or magazine.

Humans and Doorjambs

Lovebirds that are allowed to walk around on the floor are in constant danger of being stepped on or being crushed in a doorjamb. Lovebirds that are the same color as the carpeting are particularly susceptible to being crunched underfoot. Never allow your lovebird access to the floor.

Toxic Foods

Most foods are perfectly fine for a lovebird to ingest, with the exception of avocado (parts of it are toxic), chocolate, alcohol, caffeine, and raw onion. These items can make a lovebird very ill or even kill it. Junk foods, such as salty snacks or sweet deserts are not toxic, but they're not great for your lovebird either.

Electricity

Lovebirds are notorious chewers and love to snack on electric wires. Keep all wires wrapped and hidden away from your bird. Lamps and other plug-in appliances do not make good playgyms.

Heavy Metals

Keep your lovebird away from stained glass decorations, costume jewelry, lead fishing weights, or other materials containing metals that can be toxic to your lovebird. Hardware cloth, the material many people use to build cages, is often dipped in zinc to prevent rusting. Zinc is deadly for your lovebird. Rinse and scrub all homemade cage material thoroughly before housing birds.

Temperature Fluctuations

Lovebirds are sensitive to extreme heat and extreme cold. They can die from overheating and are prone to frostbite in cold, windy conditions. If you live in an extreme climate, be sensitive to your lovebird's temperature requirements. Lovebirds can stand heat to 90 degrees Fahrenheit (in the shade with a lot of cool water available) and cold to 50 degrees, but they don't prefer these extremes. A lovebird is happiest at a temperature between 70 and 85 degrees.

Mirrors and Glass
A lovebird that has full flight will not know the difference between empty space and a clean window or mirror. Your lovebird will think that he can fly right through them, and this can have drastic consequences. Many birds break their necks this way. This is a great excuse to leave your windows dirty, or at least to buy pretty decals to put on them.

Medicines
Never try to treat your bird with human medicines, which may react very differently in your bird's delicate system than they do in yours. Treat your bird only with medicines provided by your avian veterinarian and prescribed to your bird.

Lovebird-proofing Your Home
If your lovebird is going to have free time out of the cage and there is the possibility of you turning your back on it for a moment, even just to answer the phone, you'd better lovebird-proof your home. The average home presents many dangers for a lovebird. Follow this list to help to keep your feathered friend safe.

Lovebird-proofing checklist
- Screen all windows and doors and check regularly for holes in the screening.
- Wrap all electric wires and tuck them away.
- Put decals on all windows and mirrors.
- Remove all items containing toxic metals.
- Remove all toxic plants.
- Keep toilet lids down and remove all other standing water.
- Remove ceiling fans or keep them turned off.

Tips for Common Emergencies
Sometimes it's not easy to get to an avian veterinarian right away

Lovebirds are very sensitive to heat fluctuations and can die if they become overheated. Maintain your lovebirds in an environment that is between 70 and 85 degrees.

after an emergency has occurred, so you will have to comfort and treat your lovebird on your own until you can get to the doctor's office. The following is a list of tips for dealing with common emergencies.

Creating a Hospital Cage

A hospital cage is important to have on hand for many emergencies and illnesses. It's a comfortable, warm, safe place for your lovebird to calm down and recuperate from a trauma or sickness. Simply line a 10-gallon aquarium with paper towels and place a heating pad on low to medium underneath one-half of the aquarium. (Your bird must be able to move away from the heat if he gets too warm.) Cover the aquarium with a mesh aquarium cover and drape a towel over three-quarters of the tank. Place a very shallow dish of water (a weak bird can drown in even an inch of water) in the cage, as well as some millet spray and seeds or pellets. Do not include toys or perches, but you can include a rolled up hand towel for snuggling. Place the cage in a quiet location and clean the papers once a day.

Contact with Poison

If your bird comes in contact with poison and you notice evidence of vomiting, paralysis, bleeding from the eyes, nares, mouth, or vent, seizures, or shock, and you're not able to get to an avian veterinarian right away, call the National Animal Poison Control Center 24-hour Poison Hotline and ask for their help. (The telephone number is listed in the Resources section.) You will need to have an idea of the poison your bird has ingested.

Dealing with Broken Blood Feathers

Sometimes a wing or tail feather will break in the middle of the growth process and begin to bleed. This is not a serious injury, and it is one you can deal with yourself. Keep a styptic powder or pencil on hand in case of a bleeding emergency such as this one and apply the product until the bleeding has stopped. Next, you will need to remove the feather with a pair of needle-nosed pliers. While restraining the bird (you may need two people for this procedure), simply grasp the broken feather with the pliers close to the shaft, hold the wing firmly, and pull straight out. This will stop the bleeding and prevent infection. If you are too squeamish to do this yourself, take your lovebird to your avian veterinarian.

Be prepared for any emergency that may arise. Keep a hospital cage, the avian vet's phone number, and a first-aid kit on hand in case your bird becomes injured.

Oil on the Feathers

If your lovebird becomes soaked in oil, it will no longer be able to regulate his body temperature. This is a condition that can be deadly. Dust the oil-soaked bird with cornstarch or flour, and then gently bathe him in a small tub of warm water and some mild grease fighting dish soap. Don't scrub the bird. You may have to repeat this process several times. Keep the bird in a warm hospital cage until most of the oil is removed and the bird is dry.

Immediate Response to Overheating

An overheated lovebird will pant and spread his wings, trying to cool itself. If this is unsuccessful and the heat does not abate, the bird may lose consciousness and even die. If you notice that your lovebird is becoming overheated, move it to a cooler place and run a fan near the cage. Lightly mist the bird with cool water and offer drops of cool water in his mouth. Never set a lovebird out in the sun unless it has a shady spot to retreat to, and never leave a lovebird in a closed car on a warm day. Birds are easily overcome by heat.

Response to Egg-binding

Occasionally a female lovebird will become calcium deficient or have a disorder of the reproductive tract, and an egg will become stuck inside of her. This can cause paralysis and even death if left untreated. If you notice your female bird fluffed on the bottom of her cage, panting, and she has a distended belly and her droppings are large and watery, she may be trying to lay an egg. Give her some time to lay it on her own, but if 24 hours pass and she hasn't laid it, you may need to intervene.

If you can't get her to an avian veterinarian right away, place a few drops of mineral oil or olive oil in her vent (just at the outside of it) and a couple of drops in her mouth. This may help to lubricate the area and ease the egg out. If that doesn't work, try it again and move her into a very warm hospital cage and call your avian veterinarian. Even if she passes the egg, she might need an examination so that the situation doesn't occur again.

Your Lovebird's First-Aid Kit

The following is a list of essential items for a bird first-aid kit. Keep these items in a small tackle box for convenient access when you need them.

Keep a lovebird first-aid kit in the house. It should contain necessary items such as bandages, antibiotic ointment, towels, and alcohol.

Alcohol (for sterilizing tools)
Antibiotic ointment (for small wounds, use a non-greasy product)
Baby bird formula (can be used for adult birds having a difficult time eating)
Bandages and gauze
Bottled water (you may need clean, fresh water to flush out a wound or clean your bird of debris)
Cotton balls and cotton swabs
Dishwashing detergent (mild, for cleaning oil off feathers)
Electrolyte solution for human babies (for reviving a weak bird)
Eyewash
First-aid cream
Heating pad (always allow your bird the option of moving off of the heating pad)
Hydrogen Peroxide (always use in a weak solution with water)
Nail clippers
Nail file
Needle-nosed pliers (for broken blood feathers)
Penlight
Saline solution
Sanitary wipes
Sharp scissors
Small, clean towels (for holding or swabbing)
Spray bottle (for misting)
Styptic powder or pencil (to stop bleeding)
Syringe (without needle)
Transport cage
Tweezers
Veterinarian's phone number

Safe Traveling Tips

Keeping your bird safe while traveling is easy when you have the right equipment and you plan ahead. First, your bird must have a safe carrier. Consider buying a travel crate such as those made by Nylabone®. They are sturdy, come in a variety of sizes, and provide your bird with adequate ventilation. It's dangerous to transport your lovebird in its home cage. Toys and other swinging objects can injure your bird, and the multiple doors make it far easier to escape from than a carrier. Bird-specific carriers have a grating and door on the top so that the bird can

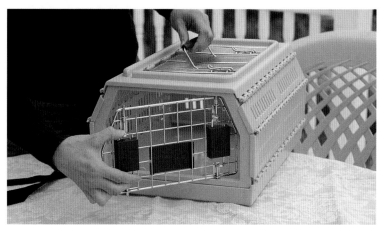

Consider purchasing a sturdy Nylabone® Fold-Away Pet Carrier to keep your bird safe when traveling.

see up instead of just out of one door. The door on top also makes it easier to catch a reluctant bird.

Most airlines will accept a bird and will allow you to keep it under your seat, though you may have to pay extra for the luxury. Call the airline first and get written permission to take your pet on the plane. If you are traveling by car, make sure that you can take your bird into the hotel. Never leave your bird unattended in a car or you might find him gone when you return. Thieves love to steal birds because they know that birds are valuable. Always take your bird-specific first-aid kit in the case of an emergency and find an avian veterinarian located at your destination spot before you leave. If you want to make life really easy on yourself, find a bird-sitter and leave your lovebird at home!

Care Sheet

In the event that you go on vacation and leave your bird with someone else, use a checklist to ensure that the bird-sitter can properly care for your bird. Make sure that the you leave the veterinarian's phone number, a number to call in case of an emergency, and detailed instructions as to what your bird eats, likes, dislikes, and other care instructions. Before you go on vacation, ask the person who will be taking care of your bird to come over and "practice" a few times to get the hang of it. This is especially important if your "baby-sitter" does not own birds.

LOVEBIRD BEHAVIOR

Birds are often difficult to understand. It sometimes seems that they come from another planet. This is likely due to the fact that our companion birds, including the lovebird, are not domesticated animals, even though lovebirds have been kept in captivity for more than 400 years. A domesticated animal is one that humans have changed through selective breeding to suit our needs. The cow, for example, can be bred to have a certain fat content in its flesh or to produce milk with certain desired components. Dogs are bred to accomplish certain tasks, such as herding or hunting vermin, and their instincts are selected and honed by breeders. Companion birds, on the other hand, have not been changed so drastically that they have lost their natural instincts. We can understand why a Border Collie herds sheep, but we have a difficult time understanding why our lovebirds want to chew the wallpaper. This behavior seems to serve no purpose.

The lovebird is an animal that acts out of pure instinct. It does not do things to spite you, nor does it do things to assist you. It merely acts out of a desire to fulfill its natural urges, whether that be chewing, chattering, or cuddling. The lovebird, in general, is a feisty, fearless creature that is loyal and territorial, and its normal behaviors can often seem bewildering to an owner who is not used to observing this special little pet. This chapter will help to take some of the confusion out of why lovebirds behave the way they do.

LOVEBIRD INTELLIGENCE

The lovebird is a smart little creature and is able to learn to do things on its own, like open the cage door to escape or dump the water dish for attention. Do not underestimate the brainpower of this bird. It might be tiny, but it's no dummy! The lovebird will learn things if it wants to, but it can be stubborn about learning things you want to teach it. This does not mean that it's a stupid bird but rather that it's a highly self-directed animal that has little instinct to please its owner, the way a larger bird, like a cockatoo, might. But that's all part of the lovebird's charm. The key is to understand your bird's limitations and to appreciate it as an individual.

Understand your lovebird's limitations and appreciate it as an individual.

VOCALIZATION

A healthy lovebird will be highly vocal around dawn and again around dusk. In the wild, dawn is the time when lovebirds are calling to one another to say, "I've made it through the night." It's like a little celebration each day. At dusk, they call one another again to say, "Here's where I've settled to roost. I'm okay." At these times you will hear your lovebird trilling and chirping. It will often stand tall on the perch and wave its wings up and down for emphasis. If you have a lone lovebird, it is calling to you at these times and will appreciate an answer. You should call back with a whistle or just say, "I'm here, everything's okay." This will help your lovebird feel secure. If you have two or more lovebirds, you will find that they are chatting to one another. If you listen closely, you will hear one bird call and the others respond.

If you are not a fan of getting up at dawn on a daily basis, you can change what time your lovebird begins to vocalize by regulating the amount of light that hits the cage. You can do this by covering the cage at night and uncovering it when you want in the morning, or by drawing dark curtains over your windows.

Lovebirds housed in pairs or colonies will squabble with one another and will make an urgent, frustrated squawking sound when they fight. You should try to come to recognize this sound so that you can break up any dissention among the flock or make sure that everything is under control. Fighting lovebirds can really injure one another and even kill a flockmate that they consider to be weak or a rival. If you ever hear screaming from one of your lovebirds, chances are that is caught in part of the cage or is being severely harassed by another bird and needs your assistance immediately.

A lovebird that is very attached to his human companion will often mimic sounds that the human makes, particularly clicking and whistling. This behavior is your lovebird attempting to connect with you, and it indicates a bird that is very attached to his owner. Lovebirds are not known to be able to mimic human speech well, but you may get a good response from trying to teach specific whistles.

A particularly uncanny ability that the lovebird has is "sleep singing." A lovebird that's napping during the day will often sing and chirp away, moving its little head up and down, while his eyes are closed and he is sound asleep. This functions to ward off predators, who are less likely to wrangle with an animal that is

Lovebirds call to each other at dawn and at dusk to "check in." A lone lovebird may call to you at these times. Answer your lovebird with a whistle, or talk to him for a few minutes.

awake. You will notice that your lovebird does not "sleep sing" at night, when doing so would call attention to itself.

BODY LANGUAGE

You can tell a lot about a how lovebird feels by his body language. Close observation of your lovebird may reveal the following types of body language.

Sleeping on one foot: This means that the lovebird is healthy and content. A lovebird sleeping on two feet may not be feeling well or may be too warm.

Feather fluffing: A quick ruffle of the feathers signifies a content bird that is releasing tension and getting ready to perform another task, such as flying or moving to the water dish. A lovebird that is sitting on a perch with his feathers fluffed may be not feeling well or might be cold. If your lovebird is fluffed and backed into a corner with its wings shaking and its beak open, it is displaying territorial behavior. Watch your fingers! This is a bird that's going to bite.

Stretching: Lovebirds stretch for the same reasons we do—to release tension, to get tired muscles moving again, and because it feels good.

Yawning: Birds yawn to clear their nasal passages. If you notice excessive yawning in your lovebird, it might indicate a health problem.

Lovebirds preen their feathers every day. This helps keep the feathers clean and in place.

A lovebird that flaps his wings while singing on his perch is a very content and happy lovebird.

Tail bobbing: A singing or chirping lovebird will have a wildly bobbing tail. If your lovebird's tail is bobbing a lot while it's resting on a perch, it could indicate a respiratory problem.

Backing up with tail wagging: A lovebird that's about to eliminate will back up a little, wag his tail, and then release! Get to know this posture if you want to avoid having to change your shirt.

Normal Behaviors

Lovebirds can do some pretty uncanny things that will look like problem behaviors, when, in fact, they are actually quite healthy and normal. Look for the following normal behaviors in your lovebird.

Preening: Preening is when your lovebird runs his beak through his feathers and makes sure they are all clean and in place. Each feather is made up of little strands that zip together like Velcro, and your lovebird spends a lot of time making sure that each feather is zipped properly. The lovebird has a gland at the base of the tail that produces oil. The lovebird gathers this oil on his beak during preening and spreads it throughout his feathers. This oil helps to keep the feathers supple and waterproof. Preening isn't just for vanity purposes.

Beak grinding: When a lovebird is sleepy and content, it will audibly grind the two parts of its beak together. Experts cannot find a distinct reason for this. Lovebirds seem to do it simply because they want to.

Beak wiping: When a lovebird eats a particularly juicy or messy meal, it will wipe its beak along the sides of his cage or on a perch, usually the concrete conditioning perch, if one is provided. This is akin to a human wiping his or her face with a napkin, and it is one reason why it's a good idea to disinfect and scrub perches weekly.

Wing flapping: Wing flapping while standing on a perch provides much needed exercise for a clipped bird. A bird that's flapping his wings might be testing out newly grown-in feathers. Wing waving while chirping is a sign of a content, happy bird that's calling out to communicate with other birds or his owner.

Door dancing: A lovebird that is allowed frequent out-of-cage time might develop a little door-dance. He will stand in front of his cage door and move back and forth, desperately trying to get your attention. This is a sign that your lovebird is well bonded to you.

Flattened posture, wings shaking: This posture means that your lovebird desperately wants something or wants to go somewhere. It is ready to take action on its desire, which may mean launching itself toward the object it wants—maybe you!

Regurgitation: As gross as it sounds, a lovebird that bobs his head in your direction may be "affectionately" regurgitating to you. This is a high compliment. Rarely will a lovebird actually vomit on you. It's more the thought that counts in this case.

Head down: A lovebird that is very bonded to you might desire a bit of head and neck scratching, and will show you this by putting his head down for you and offering you a fluffed neck. Gently rub your bird against the feathers and circle the ear openings lightly—this may cause your lovebird to yawn—then you know you're doing it right.

Chewing: Lovebirds are born (hatched!) to chew. This is a normal behavior. Don't take it as an aggressive act if your lovebird chews your signed Picasso to bits, it is just doing what its instincts tell it to do. If you want to save your priceless antiques, provide your bird with plenty of things to chew, including store-bought toys and household items, such as toilet paper rolls.

Toy aggression : Lovebirds like to argue with their toys, tossing them around the cage and being very rough on them. This is normal and does not indicate a problem.

Lovebirds love to chew on anything they can find. It is a natural behavior for them. Give your lovebird safe toys and perches to chew on.

PROBLEM BEHAVIORS

Because lovebirds are not domestic animals and their life in a home is truly a foreign experience, your pet lovebird may acquire problem behaviors that can cause some concern in an owner who doesn't understand why the behaviors are happening or how to change them. The following are a few of the common behavior issues that lovebirds face.

Biting

Lovebirds are feisty creatures and have a reputation for being nippy. A lovebird's beak is very sharp and can cause bleeding to the

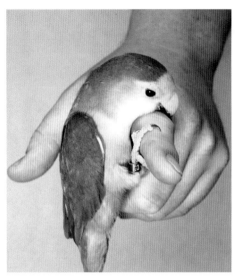

Lovebirds have a reputation for being nippy. Give your bird a "time-out" to teach him that biting is not allowed.

sensitive skin on human fingers. Females are more apt to nip because they tend to become territorial. One way to prevent biting is to play with your lovebird every day and keep him tame. If your once-tame lovebird is already biting, one way to encourage the biting is to show fear and retreat every time he gnashes his beak at you. This retreat will teach the lovebird that he is more powerful than you and that biting is a great way to get you to leave him alone.

To disarm a biting lovebird, move his cage to another room before you take him out, or gather him up in a towel and take him to a different location. This will distract the bird and allow you to play with him without being bitten. Once the bird sees that playing with you is fun, and that you're not afraid of him, the biting may cease, though this may take several weeks.

Giving a biting lovebird a "time-out," just as you would a child having a tantrum, is a good way to teach it that biting is not going to be tolerated. Simply remove the biting bird to a small "time-out" cage placed in a quiet corner. When the bird is in this cage you will not interact with him, but wait for him to calm down and compose himself. This is often an effective method of quelling biting.

Never hit a bird or flick or strike the beak in any way. A bird's beak is very sensitive, and flicking it with a fingernail hurts and can cause your bird to mistrust you. You can hold the upper part of a lovebird's beak slightly if he persists in biting, and say, "No!" firmly, though most lovebirds will continue doing what they want to do anyway. A lovebird that continues biting may not be feeling well. Look for signs of illness and take your bird to the veterinarian if you suspect something is wrong.

Territorial Display

Mature female lovebirds tend to be very territorial of the cage and will defend it by charging and gnashing at anyone who comes close. Often, females will lay eggs on the bottom of the cage and defend them like a lioness defending her cubs. Lovebirds don't seem to know that they are tiny birds, and they will attack beings far larger than themselves, like a human. In the case of a female laying infertile eggs, simply remove the eggs (you may need a glove to do this) and the bird should go back to her old, sweet self—until the next egg is laid. To play with a female that's displaying territorial behavior, you may have to remove her from the cage with a towel and take her to another room—the same prescription for biting applies. A female lovebird that's allowed to shred paper is particularly susceptible to this behavior. Remove all paper so that she doesn't think she's nesting. This territoriality is normal. It is annoying, but there's little you can do about it besides discouraging nesting behaviors.

The Jewel Thief

Lovebirds adore shiny objects and will quickly abscond with an earring—right out of your ear! It can also break a gold chain in no time and make off with the pendants. This is a normal, though annoying behavior, and can be prevented by removing jewelry before playing with the bird.

Charging

A lovebird that's very attached to one owner may not appreciate the attentions of others and may even fearlessly charge at them from across a room. To avoid this behavior, be sure to socialize your lovebird to accept the attentions of many different people.

Self-mutilation

When a lovebird is bored, confined, mistreated, has nutritional deficiencies, or has experienced a drastic change in his life, he may begin to pick out his feathers or chew other parts of his body, resulting in bleeding and bald patches. This is a terrible state for a lovebird, which uses self-mutilation as a last resort to distract itself from deplorable living circumstances. Sometimes, a lovebird that has an illness, such as a problem with the respiratory system, will pluck the feathers around the area that

Paired lovebirds display the same body language as single lovebirds, but also practice other behaviors such as allopreening and allofeeding.

disturbs it. Plucking and other mutilating behaviors always need medical attention. To prevent boredom plucking, provide your lovebird with a spacious cage and lots of different types of toys for chewing and playing.

PAIR BEHAVIOR

Lovebirds in pairs display the same body language and behaviors that single lovebirds do, but they also display certain pair behaviors as well. The following are a few behaviors that paired lovebirds are known to show.

Allopreening: Paired lovebirds will spend a good deal of time preening each other, especially in those hard-to-reach places like the top of the head and around the face.

Allofeeding: Lovebirds in pairs will feed one another, usually with the male regurgitating to the female.

Beaking: You will often find paired lovebirds playing with each other's beaks.

Chasing: Paired lovebirds are known to quibble, and you will often see the female chasing the male around or away from a certain spot in the cage.

The male mating dance: To attract females, male lovebirds do mating dance, which includes strutting along the perch and scratching his face.

Female mating posture: When a female lovebird wants to mate she will crouch down, spread her wings, and flutter them, thus enticing the male to hop on her back.

TAMING and Training Your Lovebird

I f you have a single lovebird, chances are that you will want him to be tame and come out of the cage to cuddle and play with you. You are fortunate in owning a lovebird. Once this bird is bonded to a person it is fiercely loyal and shows a deep affection for its owner. A lovebird that's bonded to its owner will beg to be let out of the cage to play, will gently preen his owner's eyebrows and hair, and will even fall soundly to sleep in the crook of its owner's neck. What a wonderful pet!

ARE LOVEBIRDS TRAINABLE?

Lovebirds are indeed trainable to do certain simple behaviors, but they are not known to be wonderful at "tricks." It's more likely that your lovebird will train you than the other way around! You will find that your lovebird will get you to do its bidding pretty quickly. Lovebirds are fast learners and they are extremely self-directed. If your lovebird is begging to be let out of his cage by making high-pitched squeaks and doing a frantic dance in front of the door and you open the cage, it will soon learn that this method works. But that's okay. It's great to have a means of communication

This is a hand-tame seagreen peach-faced. Cuddle with your bird as often as possible so he becomes used to you.

with which to understand our birds, even if that means we give in to them when they demand something.

It is unlikely that you will be able to teach your lovebird to talk, though you can try. In all my years dealing with lovebirds and their owners, I've only heard one that could talk, and I was pretty amazed! Lovebirds are better at learning whistles and clicks. They will also learn the vocalizations of other birds in the household.

HANDLING A YOUNGSTER

A very young lovebird is easy to handle. It has not yet learned to bite, and is more apt to be gentle and willing to try new things. Handle your youngster every day. Cuddle and play with it. When it begins to nip at your hands or your neck, even if the bird is just playing, stop it from nibbling and tell him, "No!" in a firm voice. There's no need to yell or make a fuss—that will just teach the bird that biting gets a reaction out of you. Little nibbles from a youngster will turn into hard biting when the bird gets a little older. Preventing bad behavior in a youngster will avoid your having to train the behavior out of the bird once it gets older. It is far easier to train a good behavior into a bird than it is to stop a bird from doing something it has gotten used to. Using the "No!" command is generally effective in stopping a behavior at the moment, but the bird often goes right back to doing what he wants to do. Keeping a close eye on your lovebird will help to prevent mischief and trouble.

TAMING AN OLDER LOVEBIRD

If you have acquired a mature, untamed lovebird, the taming and training process will take a bit of time, more so than with a youngster. There are two ways to tame a lovebird: you can "break" it or you can "gentle" it. Using a gentle, slow training method is always preferable with animals as sensitive as lovebirds. Breaking a lovebird using quick, aggressive training will work for a time but will not allow a real bond to form between you and your lovebird. Your lovebird will always be wary of you, and lovebirds have excellent memories.

Give your lovebird a period of adjustment when you first bring it home. Your bird will be stressed in its new situation and may even flutter around the cage when you approach. Do not consider taming the bird until it has settled into a routine and has come to

Taming an older lovebird may take a bit longer than taming a young bird. Be patient and gentle with your bird during training.

Give your lovebird time to get used to you and accustomed to being handled. Keep training sessions short so the bird does not become stressed.

know you and look at you without scrambling for the back of the cage. This may take a few weeks to more than a month.

When your new lovebird is adjusted to your home, you can begin taming. You will first need to clip the bird's wings. An untamed lovebird with free flight will simply fly away from you and not return. Even if you eventually want to allow your bird to fly, you will have to clip the wings during the training period—the feathers will grow back after the next molt.

THE TAMING PROCESS

Once the bird's wings are clipped, you can begin the taming process. Take your bird out of the cage with a small towel and hold him gently in the towel to prevent him from biting you. He may scream and struggle, but continue to be calm, and talk to him in a low, soothing voice. Take the bird to a small room. (A bathroom is ideal, but be sure to close the toilet lid and remove any dangerous items that may fall or break if the bird comes in contact with them.) Sit on the floor with your knees bent into "mountains" and place the bird gently on one top of your knees, holding him there for a moment before you let go. The moment you let go, the bird will probably flutter away from you in a desperate escape attempt. Gather up the bird again and try to place him on your knee again. Repeat this action until the bird eventually stands for a moment on your knee. Remember to remain calm. The bird may not want to stand on your knee during the first few sessions, but keep trying. You can do this twice a day for 20 minutes each session, but no more than that. You want to begin to build trust with the bird, not stress him out.

When your bird will stand on your knee, talk to him in a very calm voice and begin to move one hand slowly up your leg toward the bird. This may cause it to flutter off your knee again. Try again. Little by little, session after session, move your hand slowly up your leg until the bird allows it to come very close. The idea here is that the bird should eventually allow contact with your hand. This may take quite a while, so be patient. Once the bird allows your hand to approach closely, try to tickle his chest with your finger. After a few sessions of doing this, you can begin to try to get the bird to stand on your hand. Remember, all of this should be done with a lot of patience. If the bird nips your finger, don't panic or make a fuss; just keep working at this method, slowly and gently.

TRAINING "NEVERS"

There are a few things you should never do to your lovebird during training or any other time. These things will only result in breaking the trust that you and your lovebird need to build in order to have a mutually satisfying relationship.

• Never hit, flick, squeeze, or throw your lovebird. This is animal abuse and will make your lovebird mistrust you.

• Never throw anything at your lovebird's cage to make him stop chirping. Throwing things at the cage will make your lovebird feel very insecure.

• Never "play rough" with your lovebird. This will teach him to be aggressive and to bite.

• Never cover the cage for long periods during the day. If you have a sleeping infant or if you simply need your bird to quiet down, you can cover the cage for an hour or so, but it's cruel to cover the cage for extended periods when your lovebird should be active.

• Never starve your lovebird as a training tool. Sure, your bird will be hungry and might do what you want him to do for a sunflower seed, but this might backfire on you and cause your bird to become ill. Lovebirds have high metabolisms and can have seizures and even die if their blood sugar drops too low.

• Never be afraid of your lovebird. Even if you are afraid, don't show it that you are. Pulling your hand away from a bird that's bluffing a bite will teach the bird that it's powerful and that it can threaten you. Instead, use a stick or dowel to take the bird out of the cage. You should stick-train your bird as soon as possible.

TEACHING THE STEP-UP COMMAND

Of all the behaviors you can teach your lovebird, the step-up command is possibly the most important. This command allows you to retrieve your lovebird at any time, and it is especially useful when it is behaving fussy or is in potential danger. "Step-up" is when your lovebird steps gently onto your hand or finger on command. A lovebird is not hatched knowing how to do this, so you must teach it. Perhaps your lovebird came to you already tame and hand trained—that's great. But it's still important to reinforce the step-up command so that it becomes second nature to you and to your lovebird.

Assuming that you are teaching a tame or semi-tame lovebird the step-up command, begin by allowing the lovebird to come out of

Your lovebird will need to be taught how to "step-up" onto your hand or finger. This is an important command the bird should learn as soon as possible. Start out slow and take your time when training your bird.

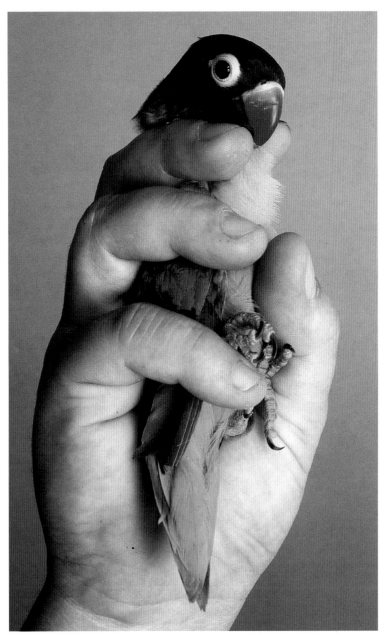

When holding your lovebird, be sure to keep a firm, but not tight, grip on him. Your bird will struggle at first, but soon will adapt to handling.

his cage on his own. You win nothing by taking the lovebird out violently and will only succeed in beginning your training session on a bad note. Place a perch on top of the cage or let the bird climb onto a standing perch where it will be standing on a round dowel, not a flat surface. If your lovebird is a youngster, you can gently lift it out of the cage, but because he doesn't yet know how to step up, be careful not to pull too hard on his feet. He will grip the perch because he doesn't understand what you want.

Once the lovebird is out of the cage, give him a treat. This can either be a bit of yummy food or a good head scratching. This will show the bird that training sessions can be fun, and it will look forward to them. Next, begin rubbing your bird's chest and belly very softly and gently with the length of your index finger, cooing to it, and slowly increasing the pressure with which you push on its chest. You may have to repeat this for a few days, depending on the tameness of your lovebird. Your semi-tame lovebird may not be sure what you are up to, and might be wary of this stroking. Take things slowly, and work to gain trust. A more tame lovebird will often sit quietly, enjoying the attention.

In time and with patience, your bird will be used to handling and let you pet him.

Once you feel that your lovebird is calm and used to this process, you can increase the pressure you place on its chest. Pushing slightly on a lovebird's chest will throw it off balance, and the bird will lift up a foot to right itself. Place your finger or hand under the foot and lift it, if the bird allows it. If not, simply allow the bird's foot to remain on your hand until the bird removes it. As you do this, tell your bird clearly to "Step-up." Always say, "Step-up" when the lovebird steps onto your hand. It's essential that your lovebird associate the action of stepping onto your hand with the phrase.

Once your lovebird is fairly good at stepping up, you can have him step from finger to finger, repeating the phrase "Step-up" and praising it. Your bird may hesitate at first, but soon he will know exactly what you want. Be sure that your training sessions last only a few minutes, and try not to become frustrated if your lovebird doesn't do exactly what you want right away. Training sessions are ideally short, perhaps 10 to 15 minutes twice a day, and should be incorporated into playtime.

Most youngsters will learn the step-up command easily, in one or two short sessions; a semi-tame lovebird will take longer. The more your lovebird trusts you, the easier it will be to teach it anything. Remember, patience is essential. Even if this command is the only "trick" you teach your lovebird, it is by far the most valuable. If you say, "Step-up" every time you lift your lovebird, you will reinforce this important training every day and make life much easier for both of you.

STICK TRAINING

Stick training is simply teaching the "step-up" command using a perch or dowel instead of your finger. It is very important that your lovebird know how to step onto a stick. The day may come when your lovebird refuses to come down from the curtain rod or gets out of the house and is sitting high in a tree, chirping away. A lovebird that has been stick trained will be easy to retrieve with a long dowel or broomstick. A lovebird that is not used to stepping on a stick will be terrified of it and you may lose the opportunity to save your bird from harm. Teach "step-up" with a stick the same way you teach it with your finger. Stick training should begin as soon as you begin hand taming your lovebird. If your bird is terrified of the stick, you can leave it close to the cage where your bird will have a chance to view it and get used to its presence. Use different sticks during training so that your lovebird learns not to be afraid of various dowels and perches.

GROOMING Your Lovebird

I t might seem strange to think about grooming your lovebird since lovebirds do much of their own grooming and keep all of their feathers tidy and in place. A healthy lovebird has a strict regimen of cleanliness. It will frequently preen its feathers and make sure that no debris lodges on its feet or beak. Preening is a very normal behavior for a healthy lovebird, one that you can encourage through regular bathing. For your part, grooming a bird includes clipping the flight feathers, keeping the toenails trimmed, and making sure that the beak is properly aligned and isn't growing too long.

ALL ABOUT FEATHERS

Feathers began on certain dinosaurs. They were the first "birds," millions of years ago. Feathers are a bird's sole source of protection from water and the cold. Well-groomed feathers protect the bird against moisture and chilly weather. Birds typically have high body temperatures, and their feathers help to keep them warm. You may notice your lovebird puffing its feathers when the temperature drops, or when it's not feeling very well. Feathers are also used to attract the opposite sex and to indicate sexual maturity. It's no wonder that your lovebird spends so much time preening and making sure every feather is in the proper place.

There are several types of feathers on your lovebird.

Contour feathers: These are the feathers that outline a lovebird's body, including the flight feathers and the feathers covering the body (coverts).

Flight feathers: The wing is comprised of 20 flight feathers: 10 primary flight feathers (the long feathers at the end of the wing) and 10 secondary flight feathers (closer to the body).

Semiplume feathers: The tiny feathers around your lovebird's beak, nares, and eyes.

Down feathers: The undercoat of fluffy feathers beneath the contour feathers. These help to insulate the lovebird and keep it warm.

WING CLIPPING

Clipping a bird's wings is the act of cutting the primary flight feathers (only the first half of the feather) so that the bird is unable

Feathers serve many purposes and are a bird's source of protection from water and cold. A bird that is too cold will fluff or puff his feathers to stay warm. Lovebirds also use their feathers to attract mates.

to fly very high or very far. These are the only feathers that you should ever clip. While wing clipping is a common and accepted practice, there is some evidence that clipping a bird's wings does frustrate the bird and can create some health problems if the bird is not active enough. Clipped lovebirds can become overweight. The same is true for lovebirds kept in tiny cages. Wild lovebirds spend most of their day flying around, looking for food and a safe place to sleep. That's a lot of exercise. A clipped bird will usually sit around all day picking out of its food dish unless you give it something to do with its time. You should make an extra effort to offer activities to a clipped lovebird. Playgyms, lots of toys, safe branches to chew, and blocks of safe, soft wood are all fun activities that will get your lovebird moving.

To Clip or Not to Clip

If you feel guilty about having your bird's wings clipped, you're not alone. Many people feel that wing clipping is cruel, or that it hurts the bird. In truth, clipping wings, if done properly, hurts as much as a haircut. Feathers, like hair, grow back in about five months if the bird is healthy, perhaps even sooner.

Should you clip your lovebird's wings? That depends more on your ideas about living with a companion bird than it does on your

Should you clip your lovebird's wings? Some bird owners prefer to leave their pets "fully flighted" as flying is good exercise and natural behavior for birds.

If you clip your lovebird's wings, make sure you give him lots of exercise and attention. Some birds will develop self-destructive behavior if they feel vulnerable or stressed.

lovebird. No bird wants its wings clipped. Birds are creatures of boundless space. Most would take the first opportunity to dash out the window for a bit of soaring time. But then what? Your lovebird lands in a tree and sees hawks circling overhead. Your lovebird's flying fun has now become a tragic situation. If your lovebird escapes, you may never find him again. And that's only one danger to keeping a lovebird flighted. Fully flighted birds are more likely to burn themselves on a hot stove, drown in the toilet, or break their necks flying headlong into clean, closed windows or shiny mirrors.

Beginner pet bird owners often keep their birds safer (alive) when their birds' wings are clipped. Will your lovebird really suffer if it is not allowed to fly? Not if you give it a lot of free time out of the cage and house it in a large space. However, flying is essential for the psychological well-being of a bird. This is an animal that is meant to fly, and when that's taken away, it can result in neurotic behaviors, such as self-mutilation. The bird will feel vulnerable and have little self-direction. Unfortunately, clipping is important for the safety of most lovebirds.

One way to avoid neurotic behavior in your clipped lovebird is to give it as much attention as possible. You may also want to consider an aviary or habitat where you birds can fly without risk. Many lovebird owners use this option and their birds are healthy and happy as a result.

Another option is to clip your new bird for an initial period of time, say six months to a year, until you and your bird come to know each other very well. This initial unflighted period will allow your bird to become used to you and your home, to your other pets, and the other family members. You must come to know and trust your bird's habits before you make the decision to let the flight feathers grow out. Remember, the potential for tragedy is always there. If you can make your home absolutely safe, and you're positive that it can't escape or injure himself in any fashion, let it fly under supervision. If you are not certain about your bird's safety, keep it clipped, but go the extra mile to provide the freedom and stimulation that it would otherwise get from flying.

How to Clip Your Lovebird's Wings

If you've chosen to clip your lovebird's wing feathers to prevent it from flying away, you should find a professional in your area that will clip them at first and show you how to do it yourself. Many owners are squeamish about clipping their own lovebird's wings, and choose to have someone else do it for them. If you have an avian veterinarian, he or she is the best person to clip your lovebird's wings. That way you have bonus of a veterinarian handling your bird. You can always clip the wings yourself and may want to learn how, especially with a lovebird, which needs the new feathers trimmed as they grow in.

Have an experienced bird keeper or avian veterinarian show you how to clip your lovebird's wings before you try it yourself.

When clipping wings, the first thing you must be able to do is hold your lovebird properly. You can't grab a bird any way you want, spread out a wing, and clip away. This can be very dangerous and lead to injury. A lovebird has fragile bones that can break if you're too rough or don't hold it properly. A bird has a different way of breathing than we do, and it's possible to prevent it from breathing by holding it around the chest area, even lightly. You should grasp the bird around the neck and the back, leaving the chest free. Your thumb is on one side of the bird's neck, bracing the bottom of its jaw, and your index finger is on the other side, doing the same. The lovebird should look like it's resting with his back in your palm. Of course your lovebird will be struggling, so you can place a washcloth over his feet so he can grasp onto it. A bird that tends to bite can be grasped like this using a thin towel so he can chew on it and not on your fingers.

Once you feel that you're holding your lovebird in the proper fashion, have someone else gently extend its wing and clip the first ten feathers (the long ones at the end of the wing), beginning at the point where the primary feather coverts end—those are the feathers on the upper side of the wing that end at the midpoint of the primary flight feathers. With a sharp pair of scissors, clip each feather, one by one, making a clean snip. Clip both wings; if you don't, your lovebird will fly in circles and become flustered and clumsy.

Don't clip your lovebird's wings until you've watched someone do it in person and have had them show you how to hold your bird properly and which feathers to clip. Don't take a pair of sharp scissors to your bird's wings unless you're sure of what you're doing.

MOLTING

When birds molt, they shed their feathers and make way for new ones to grow. The old feathers may have become ragged and not useful for insulation or flying anymore. A molt can happen once or twice a year, depending on the amount of light and warmth your lovebird is exposed to, and it is a very stressful time for a bird. Your lovebird may become ill-tempered and not want to be touched at certain times. The newly growing feathers can be uncomfortable or tender. You will notice little "pins" beginning to poke out from between your lovebird's other feathers. These are called pin feathers. The "pin" is a sheath of material (keratin) that protects the new

Molting occurs once or twice a year. Your lovebird will not shed his old feathers all at once. Molting can take several months to be complete.

feather until it is ready to emerge. Your lovebird will spend time removing these sheaths but will not be able to remove the ones on its head. If your bird allows head scratching, you can gently remove them just as a mate would.

Molting birds do not lose all of their feathers at once. Most molts are many weeks or months long, and feathers are replaced gradually. If you notice bald patches on your lovebird's body or its feathers become so thin you can see the skin beneath them, take your bird to your avian veterinarian right away because there may be a serious problem.

Pin feathers and new feathers that have just emerged from the sheath have a blood supply and will bleed if injured or broken. This often happens with a wing feather, especially in a clipped bird, which does not have fully grown wing feathers that would protect a new feather from breaking. If you notice a bleeding feather,

perhaps one that was clipped during wing trimming, don't panic. Pull the feather straight out from the root with one quick motion and the bleeding will stop immediately. A pair of needle-nosed pliers is good for this purpose, and should be kept in your bird first-aid kit. If you're squeamish about this, apply styptic powder to the bleeding area and take your bird to your avian veterinarian as soon as possible.

CARE FOR THE MOLTING LOVEBIRD

Molting is a stressful time for a lovebird and it will need special care to make this time more comfortable. Regular misting with warm water is helpful in softening the pin feathers. Only mist your bird in temperate weather and

You may need to trim your bird's toenails a few times a year. The avian veterinarian can show you how to do this if you are uncertain.

Do all you can to keep your lovebird in the best of health. Your bird is relying on you for all his needs.

when there's adequate time for it to dry before evening. Offer your lovebird an extra-nutritious diet while he's molting, including a protein source, such as hard-boiled eggs, egg food, and boiled chicken. You shouldn't notice any difference in the way your lovebird behaves, eats, plays, or responds to you during a molt, but there is the possibility for it to behave differently while the new feathers are emerging.

TRIMMING THE TOENAILS

If you play with your lovebird regularly, you might notice that its toenails pinch and prick you. This is the time to trim the bird's toenails. If your lovebird has a conditioning perch made of concrete or another rough material, you may only have to trim the toenails three or four times a year. Your lovebird's toenails should have a graceful half-moon curve to them, if they extend beyond this, your bird might have a medical problem related to a nutritional deficiency, or it could potentially have mites. See your veterinarian if your lovebird's toenails seem unusual in any way.

A bird's toenails are like our toenails; there's a dead part and a living part, called the quick. When trimming your bird's nails you only want to cut off the dead part of the nail. Cutting into the quick is very painful and causes bleeding. Trim the nails very conservatively.

In a bird with clear or pink nails, it will be easy to see the quick and avoid cutting into it. In a bird with dark nails you will only want to take off the very tip of the nail. You can use a nail clipper (the kind used for babies) to trim the nails, which may be a two-person job—one to hold the bird properly and one to trim the nails. If bleeding does occur, simply apply styptic power to the wound and it should stop.

SHOULD I GROOM THE BEAK?

There should never be a reason for you to groom your lovebird's beak. Eating hard items, chewing toys, and grooming the beak on a conditioning perch will all help to keep the beak trimmed and aligned properly. In some cases, when a lovebird is ill or has a severe nutritional deficiency or mites, the beak may become elongated and may interfere with eating. This is a case for a veterinarian's treatment. You can severely injure your lovebird by trying to trim the beak yourself.

BATHING YOUR LOVEBIRD

If you offer your lovebird water in a coop cup, it will bathe itself and splash water all over the cage and surrounding area. A bathing lovebird is fun to watch. It gets in the water belly first and flips the water everywhere with its wings and head—a messy occasion! You can offer a special shallow bath that attaches to a cage door and allows the lovebird to enter and splash around, or you can simply set a shallow pan of water in or near your lovebird's cage—your lovebird will know what to do. Some very tame lovebirds will enjoy bathing in a soft stream of water coming from the kitchen sink's tap, or will even enjoy sitting on a special perch while their owner is showering. A mister simulating rain is a good way to get your lovebird to bathe.

Bathing is important for your lovebird not only because it keeps the bird clean, but also because it encourages preening. You bird only needs clean, fresh water for bathing. There are bathing products that you can buy from the pet shop, but they are unnecessary. Bathe your bird only in warm weather and in the daytime, allowing plenty of time for it to dry thoroughly. Never use soaps or other detergents to bathe your lovebird—plain, fresh water will do.

BREEDING Your Lovebird

Part of the reason for the lovebird's popularity (especially the peach-faced, the Fischer's, and the masked species), is that they breed eagerly and the chicks appear in the nest box in a wide variety of colors. The peach-faced lovebird in particular breeds so readily that it is considered the "rabbit" of the bird world. The ease in breeding these birds makes them a good choice for newcomers to the hobby of aviculture. It can be frustrating to try to breed birds that are reluctant or behave badly to their babies, but you won't have a tenth of these problems with the lovebird.

Learning the science behind the genetic mutations of the lovebird also makes it a fascinating species to breed. Even the novice breeder can come to understand the basic genetic makeup of the lovebird and be able to breed for specific colors. Paying close attention to the genetics of lovebird breeding might seem like a "mad scientist" way of propagating the species, but it is the way most serious lovebird breeders operate.

SHOULD YOU BREED YOUR LOVEBIRD?

Breeding birds is not an activity that should be entered into lightly. It's a hobby that produces living creatures. It's sometimes hard to find a suitable home for an animal. The first thing you should consider is what you will do with the babies your pair produces. You have a few options: you can keep them if you have the room; you can give them away as gifts to people who want them; you can sell the babies if you are able to let go of them once you've become attached to them; you can trade them with another lovebird breeder for color mutations you want if you desire to keep breeding. Do you have the time to care for many more birds than you already own? There may be a lot of cages to clean. How will you sell the babies? You might have to take out a classified ad and allow strangers to come to your home or sell them to a pet shop where you will be unsure of where they will live out their lives.

Next, you have to consider the fact that you might lose your beloved pet to another partner—its bird-mate. Your sweet cuddlebug will no longer want to play and be friendly with you when she's sitting on a clutch of eggs. She might return to her former self once

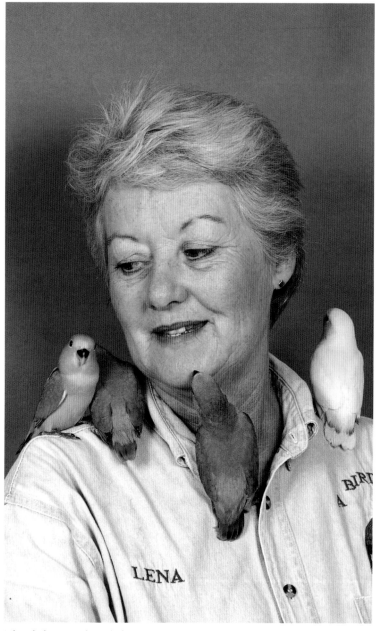

These baby normal peach-faced and lutino peach-faced are very friendly as a result of being handfed.

Breeding lovebirds takes time and dedication. Consider all the factors involved before you breed your birds. These Fischer's lovebirds are two weeks old.

the babies have fledged (left the nest), but that's not always the case. Also, you might risk losing her to breeding complications such as egg-binding or calcium deficiency. Can you deal with a parent bird or hatchling dying because of something you forgot to do or because of something you did by mistake? Think carefully before you set a pet bird up for breeding.

Breeding also brings an extra expense and takes a great deal of time, especially if you're going to hand-feed the babies yourself. You will have to buy breeding equipment, perhaps visit the veterinarian, and be prepared for anything that goes wrong—and things will go wrong. Even the best-laid plans don't always pan out in the bird-breeding biz.

Finally, think about bringing all those new lives into the world when there are so many birds today that become unwanted and are placed up for adoption. Some beginning breeders think that they will sell their babies and use the money to help pay the expenses they incur caring for their birds. This seems like a logical plan, but breeding always costs more than you think it will. One veterinary visit alone can eat up all of your profits.

If you still want to breed your lovebirds once you know the potential downfalls, at least you're prepared. Breeding lovebirds can be an entertaining and rewarding hobby, especially when you begin to cultivate relationships with other lovebird breeders to share information and stories of breeding success. There can be a real camaraderie between hobbyists, and that's a large part of the fun.

PAIRING UP

The first item on your list for breeding is a pair of lovebirds. If you're breeding one of the three popular monomorphic species (peach-faced, Fischer's, or masked), it may be difficult to determine if you have a true pair because you will not be able to tell the difference between the male and the female. There are some telltale signs you can look for, however, when trying to determine sex in mature birds.

• The female of the species is generally a bit larger in length and girth than the male, and she is often heavier.

• The female is feistier than the male and quicker to cause squabbles with another bird. Males tend to be more docile.

• The female is extremely interested in tearing and shredding paper and other nesting materials than the male.

• The female peach-faced lovebird will tuck strips of paper into the feathers of her rump and transport them to the nest. Males do not tuck. A sure way of finding the mature females in a group of lovebirds is to provide a piece of newspaper or a palm frond and record which birds chew it into strips and tuck it into their rump.

• Female Fischer's and masked lovebirds go into high gear nesting behavior when a nest and nesting material is present and transport material to the nest using the beak.

• Males regurgitate to females. Females can sometimes exhibit this behavior, but not as often as males.

• Females tend to have wider pelvic bones. If you can place your index finger between the pelvic bones (right at the area of the vent) and they feel thick and blunt, you might have a female; if the pelvic bones feel narrow and pointy, you might have a male.

If you're still wondering about your "pair" there are three sure fire ways of determining if you have a male and a female. First, you can simply set them up with a nest box and see what happens. If they have babies, then you have a pair! If they produce dozens of unfertile eggs, you have two females going to

Before you can breed your lovebirds, you must make certain that you have a breeding pair. These are creamino pied peach-faced and lutino pied peach-faced lovebirds.

nest. If they produce no eggs and the birds only use the nest for sleeping, you may have two males.

Another way of determining sex is to have your avian veterinarian perform a short surgery on your lovebirds. The doctor inserts a small scope into the bird's abdomen and looks inside to view the sexual organs. This procedure is costly and can be dangerous for the bird, which must undergo anesthesia for the procedure. You can have your birds sexed by providing a bit of their DNA, either a blood sample or a feather, to a lab who will use it to determine the sex of your bird. This technology is very effective and fairly inexpensive.

BREEDING EQUIPMENT AND SETUP

Once you determine that you have a breeding pair, you will want to set up the pair properly so that you get the maximum number of babies while still keeping your lovebirds happy and healthy. The first thing you will need to do is condition your pair for breeding. This means that you will make your birds as healthy and as nutritionally fortified as possible before you set them up to breed. Because lovebirds don't have a set breeding season (you can set them up any time of year depending on the weather), you can afford to take two or three months to bulk up your birds. For a few months before you breed them, you will provide your pair with a roomy space in which to get a lot of exercise, and offer them a bounty of

If you decide to breed your lovebirds, you'll have to provide the breeding pair with an appropriate nest box. This is a peach-faced lovebird nest.

fresh foods, especially those rich in calcium and Vitamin A. Provide a cuttlebone and mineral block, and sprinkle calcium powder on everything they eat.

Your breeding cage should be a minimum of 3-feet long, 2-feet wide, and 18-inches to 2-feet tall. A nesting hen needs a good deal of exercise to keep healthy. A hen that's confined can become eggbound and have other breeding problems that can lead to death.

The peach-faced lovebird will nest in a square wooden box, approximately 6 or 7 inches by 7 or 8 inches, by 8 to 10 inches tall; an eye ring lovebird likes a nest box that's longer and skinnier. The peach-faced lovebird doesn't make much of a nest, but the eye ring species will make quite a home for their eggs, and will even build two rooms inside the nest, one compartment for the eggs and one for sleeping. Clip a hole in the cage that is big enough to match up with the hole in the nest, and hang the nest outside of the cage if it's safe to do so. If it's not safe, and the cage is large enough, you can hang the box inside the cage, though it will be more difficult for you to get to when the babies are hatched. You can hang it with cup hooks or other safe hardware.

Be sure to secure the outside doors of the nest box because some lovebirds are crafty enough to figure out how to remove the doors and escape. Place a perch near the nest hole so the birds can get in and out easily. This perch is also the place where the male bird will keep his sentry position. Fill the nest up to the hole with pine shavings (not cedar). The peach-faced will kick some of these shavings out, and the eye ring species will remove most of them. The shavings give the birds the feeling of making a nest and provide insulation for the eggs and material for the babies' feet to grasp. Provide your pair with nesting material such as white newsprint paper, clean cornhusks, and clean palm fronds (a favorite).

Once your pair is beginning to nest, leave them alone. Don't fuss around the nest or add anything to it. Your birds know what they're doing.

Colony Breeding

Lovebirds breed well in a colony situation if they are provided with enough space, nest boxes, and feeding stations. Six pairs are the minimum for a colony. Strangely enough, two female lovebirds are likely to fight, while three or more will get along better. Always hang the nest boxes as high as possible in a colony and provide at least two

Lovebirds can breed well in a colony. Be sure to offer many different sized nest boxes and feeding stations to prevent squabbling. This is a colony of peach-faced mutations.

extra nest boxes so that there will be no fighting over the "best" ones. Offer a few feeding stations so that the more timid pairs aren't afraid to eat. You will not be able to correctly determine the parentage of the babies hatched in a colony situation. Lovebirds do mate for life, but they are known to have a dalliance every now and then. Babies fledging in a colony situation are in danger of being picked on, so be sure to remove them soon after they are ready to leave the nest, or plan on hand-feeding your babies.

BREEDING AND NESTING BEHAVIORS

When your female is done setting up her nest and making it comfortable, she will spend a lot of time inside the box, allowing the male to feed her and provide security. He will rarely enter the box but will if she lets him. About ten days after mating, she will lay an egg about every other day until there are about five to six eggs in the box. The number of eggs can vary, and it's not unusual to have a clutch of eggs numbering fewer than five or more than ten. The male will stand outside of the box, and make sure that everything is okay. Don't be concerned if you don't see the female a lot, though there is cause for concern should you see her too much—this might mean she's not sitting on the eggs as much as she should. How long she sits on the eggs per day depends a lot on the weather and humidity. The male never sits on the eggs, though he will sleep in the nest if the female allows him inside.

You can check on the eggs if you want, but do so only if you suspect that your female will allow this without becoming so disgruntled that she abandons her eggs, though lovebirds aren't likely to do that. A hand-fed hen will have no issue with attacking fingers. A parent-raised hen that

Although the male never sits on the eggs, the female may allow him to sleep in the nest and to check on the eggs. Try not to disturb the female when she is tending to her eggs.

has never had a human pal will be more likely to scuttle off the eggs for you to take a look. Beginners to the hobby often bother their hens too much. Try to restrain yourself from looking in the nest box too often. Peeking in once a day should be sufficient.

Breeding Timeline

Once all of the eggs are laid, the female will begin to sit tight on them for an incubation period of between 21 to 25 days, depending on the weather. It might take less time for the babies to hatch in a hot climate and a few more days in a cold climate. The babies will hatch in the order that the eggs were laid. If there are six fertile eggs

The female lovebird will incubate her eggs for 21 to 25 days, depending on the weather. The eggs will hatch in the order in which they were laid.

in the clutch, you can expect that the oldest baby will be at least ten days older, maybe more, than the last baby, who may be crushed by its older siblings. In this case, consider pulling the first three babies out of the nest when they are around two weeks old, and hand-feed them so that the younger babies have sufficient room and attention.

Babies will leave the nest and wean at around eight to nine weeks of age. They will still want to sleep in the nest, but the female, who likely has another clutch of eggs to sit on, will beat them fiercely and send them packing. Remove the young from the parents immediately after they are weaned.

DETERMINING IF EGGS ARE FERTILE

To find out if your hen has laid fertile eggs, you can "candle" them to see what's inside the fragile shell when they are about a week old. You can use a flashlight as a rudimentary candler—simply turn it on and place the eggs, one by one, on to the face of the flashlight so that the light shines through. An unfertile egg will be clear and a fertile egg will have red veins running through it and show a visible dark spot inside. As the bird develops inside the egg, you can see its body kicking and rolling. A day or so before hatching, you will be able to hear the chick cheeping loudly from inside the egg. If you have an ornery hen and the flashlight method doesn't work for you, buy a commercial candler that has a wand attached to the flashlight so that you don't have to touch to eggs. If you are viewing the eggs regularly and you notice a hairline fracture, you can repair it by painting the fracture with a very light coat of clear nail polish or a thin sheen of white glue, but don't be surprised if that particular egg doesn't hatch.

Breeding Problems

When the breeding process goes smoothly it is a joy to be a part of; but when there are problems with the parents, eggs, or babies, it can be a heartbreaking and frustrating experience. The following are a few of the problems associated with breeding lovebirds.

Egg-binding

A hen that's not fit to breed, has too small of a cage, or has a medical problem, can become egg-bound. This means that the egg is stuck inside her and won't come out. This is a serious condition that can lead to paralysis and death. You can tell that a hen is "eggnant" when she has a distended abdomen and her droppings become large and watery. If she doesn't pass the egg in a couple of

A fertile egg will have red veins running through it. A day or so before the eggs hatch, you will be able to hear the chicks peeping inside the eggs.

days, or if you notice that she has become lame, take her to your veterinarian immediately.

Calcium Deficiency

A hen that's calcium deficient can have eggs that crumble inside of her. This can lead to a serious medical condition that causes her bones to become brittle, or she will lay fertile eggs that collapse on the babies, causing them to die. To prevent this condition, provide your pair with plenty of calcium-rich foods and supplements.

Poor Parenting

Lovebirds are usually doting parents, but there's the occasional hen that abuses her babies, eating or mauling them when they leave the shell. You won't know that your hen is a mauler until she does this to a clutch. Once you are aware of her propensity to abuse her chicks, you can remove the eggs and place them under another hen or incubate them yourself.

Too Many Babies

Sometimes a hen is so good, she will lay ten or more fertile eggs and try to raise all of the babies. Not only will this exhaust her, the older babies will likely crush the younger babies. Remove the first half of the babies and hand-feed them yourself, allowing the hen to raise the other half of the clutch.

Dead-in-shell

Lack of moisture and temperature fluctuations, among other things, can cause dead-in-shell babies. Offer your pair a water dish that they can bathe in. The hen will often wet her breast feathers to take moisture into the nest.

Splay Leg

If a baby doesn't have anything to grasp on the bottom of the nest box, it can develop a condition known as splay leg, where its legs flair out to the side of the bird instead of straight down. This bird will not be able to perch well, and is considered handicapped. To prevent splay leg, make sure the babies have something to grasp with their feet, such as pine shavings. Wrapping gauze around the bird's legs and taping them together for a short period of time can often correct splay leg. Consult your veterinarian before you do this yourself.

Unfortunately, not all breeding programs are completely successful. Sometimes there can be problems with the baby birds or the parents. These are healthy peach-faced nestlings.

Parent and Baby Nutrition

Parent birds need a nutritious diet while they are feeding babies. This diet is going to fortify the young and make them grow, so you want it to be as healthy and balanced as possible. Include all of the foods you fed to condition the pair, but add crushed hardboiled egg and egg food, as well as soaked pellets, bird biscuits, and millet spray. Soft foods are important at this time.

Hand-raising Babies

Most lovebird breeders hand-feed their baby lovebirds and make them tame for the pet market. Hand-feeding is easy once you get the hang of it, but it can also be deadly to the babies if you don't know what you're doing. You can choke the babies if the formula goes down the windpipe. The crop (holding area for the stomach) can burn if the food is too hot or become soured if the food is too cool.

The ideal time to remove lovebird babies from the nest is at about two weeks, or after their eyes have opened. Place them in a small fish tank or other container that they can't tip over or escape from as they grow older. Fill the container with pine shavings and line the bottom with paper towels. Place a heating pad underneath half of the container so that the babies can move away from the heat if they become too warm. Cover most of the container with a dark towel, but make sure that the babies can still get fresh air. If you can invest in a professional brooder, do so. A very young chick should be kept at around 97 degrees Fahrenheit and an older chick that is "feathering out" should be kept at around 95 degrees. These are the best temperatures for the proper digestion of food.

Feeding

There are many good hand-feeding formulas on the market. Choose the one you like and prepare it following the directions on the package. You can feed the babies using a variety of implements: a syringe (without the needle), a pipette, an eyedropper, or a bent spoon. Novices should try the eyedropper first because it's very easy to feed too quickly with the syringe, forcing food down the windpipe and choking the babies. The spoon is an easy option as well, but it can result in beak deformities when used by a novice.

Once you've prepared the formula, mix it well to ensure that it's the same temperature throughout, place the tip of the feeding implement to the side of the beak to encourage a feeding response. The baby lovebird should "pump" the implement eagerly. Never try to force-feed a baby bird. As the bird pumps, squeeze the formula slowly into its beak. This takes patience and a gentle hand. The baby is full when its crop looks full and when it's satiated. Never feed a baby to bursting—this can lead to crop problems and choking. Two-week old babies should be on a four-hour feeding schedule, but as they get older you can cut back the feedings until they are weaned.

Hand-feeding baby lovebirds will wean at between eight to ten weeks of age. Around seven to eight weeks you can begin offering them a wide variety of foods and a dish of water. Soft foods and "fun" foods, like cereal, are easy to eat. Never discontinue feedings until you are sure that the babies are eating well on their own.

The following is a list of a few of the many problems can go wrong during the hand-feeding process.

Crop burn: If your formula is too hot, or has "hot spots" because you're using the microwave to heat it, the food can actually burn the crop and the baby can die.

A hand-fed baby lovebird should be weaned at about eight to ten weeks of age. Make sure the babies are feeding on their own before you discontinue feeding. This is a good example of a young orange face peach-faced lovebird.

Infection: Clean all of your feeding implements thoroughly after use, and toss the unused formula after each feeding. These items can harbor bacteria and can cause a deadly infection in the babies.

Respiratory problems: It's easy to choke (aspirate) a baby bird in an instant. Feed slowly. Sometimes, an eager hand-feeder will force too much food down the bird's throat, causing little bits of it to enter the respiratory tract, eventually causing pneumonia.

Poor socialization: A hand-feeder must take care to properly socialize the chicks. This means offering them gentle attention and handling.

BANDING BABIES

You might notice a closed band around your parent lovebirds' legs. This is an identification band that tells where the bird was hatched, in what year, by what breeder, and it has a unique number that the breeder has kept for their records. Some states require this band in order for you to sell your babies. You can purchase the bands through a lovebird society or through an ad in a bird magazine. Band your babies when they are under two weeks old by lubricating the band and inserting the two front toes first, with the back two following. There is usually no problem with placing the babies back in the nest with the hen; however, some hens are offended by the band and will chew their youngsters' feet off to remove them.

RESTING YOUR PAIR

You should rest your pair after they have had three clutches, giving them a few months to bulk up again. If you live in a hot climate, rest your birds during the summer. If you live in a cold climate, rest them during the winter. This rest will prevent egg-binding, calcium deficiency, and will ensure strong babies in the clutches after the resting period.

A SHORT COURSE IN LOVEBIRD GENETICS

As you may have noticed, peach-faced lovebirds come in what seems like an endless array of colors. The eye ring species shows a variety of beautiful mutations as well. A trip to a bird show or expo should give you a good indication of how many different combinations of lovebird colors are available. There are at least 17 distinctive mutations to date in the peach-faced alone, and more are discovered each year.

A color mutation is a color in the feathers of a bird that is different from the "nominate" color, or the color most found in the wild. For example, the green, or "normal," lovebird is the color most found in nature, the color most able to camouflage itself in the wild terrain of Africa, where being a bright attractive color could be dangerous. In captivity, where a bright attractive color is desirable for the lovebird owner, the mutated color genes survive. Note that a color mutation in lovebirds is different than hybridization. Hybridization is when two different species of lovebirds are mated, sometimes creating birds known as "mules," or unfertile babies. This is not recommended and is, in fact, strongly discouraged by the bird community.

It 1856, in Brunn, Austria, a monk named Gregor Mendel began a study of garden pea plants, the coloring in their blossoms, the shapes of their seeds, and the properties of their leaves. After many years of research on many generations of pea plants, Mendel concluded that the visible alternative characteristics appear due to what we now call genes. Sixteen years after Mendel's death, his remarkable study was found, retested, and designated Mendel's

This is a creamino lovebird mutation. Note the band on the foot.

Law. It changed genetics forever. Mendel's method of determining color in offspring works perfectly on lovebirds.

For this very short section on genetics, we're going to look at the peach-faced lovebird, because it has the most variety of mutations to date.

First, the basics: green is the nominate color for peach-faced lovebirds, the next common color being a hue close to blue. Even when a bird is outwardly not green or blue, such as the bright yellow lutino, or the buttery-yellow creamino, they still fall under the green and blue mutation categories. It's hard to see a yellow bird as "green," but it still falls in the green category. A lovebird's external color is not always indicative of the other genes it carries. A gene is the part of the chromosome that determines what characteristics an organism will have. Some genes are dominant and some are recessive. When a lovebird's visual color is a dominant color, green for example, we call the bird "normal." When the bird visually shows a recessive color, we call it bird a "visual split."

For example, the color lutino (yellow) is recessive, so when a lovebird is lutino, we say that it is "visually split to lutino." The male lovebird is the parent that carries the genes that will show up visually in the babies (unless the gene is sex-lined, but we'll get to that in a moment).

The word "split" is used to indicate that a male bird is carrying other genetic traits than the one that's showing visually in his appearance. Females cannot be split, though they do carry sex-linked genes that will show up visually in offspring. So, a green male lovebird can be "split to" lutino. He will not show any appearance of being lutino, but he will have inherited the genes for lutino from one of his parents. When this green (split to lutino) male is bred, a certain percentage of his offspring will be visually lutino. So, it follows that a green male with all green genes that is mated to a lutino (yellow) female will produce all green babies. Green is dominant to yellow, so green "wins." The male offspring from that pairing will be "split" to lutino, meaning that they will be visually green, but will have inherited the yellow gene from their mother and will be able to pass it on to their offspring. If one of these "split to lutino" babies were mated to a lutino hen, both green and lutino babies will result. It would take a lutino male that has all of his genes set for lutino and a lutino hen to create offspring that are all lutino.

Much of determining what color babies you will get is about first determining what genes the parents are carrying that are "dominant." A dominant gene, such as the gene for the color green, will always win over a recessive gene, unless there's something in the background of both of the parents that will change the color in some way, usually in the next generation (the grandchicks).

For example, the gene for the trait "cinnamon" must be carried by the hen (a sex-linked gene) in order for it to be passed to the male offspring, who in turn will not show cinnamon, but will pass it on visually to their babies. The gene for pied is dominant and will show up in most of the offspring, no matter which parent is carrying it. For example, a baby may be heavily pied or just have one toe or one feather that indicates the presence of the gene, but it still shows up visually. Often, a bird carrying the pied gene will have an uneven line where its face color meets its body color, and this might be the only indication of the pied gene being carried by that particular bird.

Confused yet? You will learn through experimentation and through talking to other breeders how to determine the colors of your babies. By far, the best way to determine what genes your birds are carrying is to keep fastidious records about your flock and their offspring. When you first begin breeding lovebirds (unless you buy them from reputable breeders who keep excellent records), you will not be able to determine what genes your lovebirds carry until you breed them and then breed their babies. If you want immediate results and you have the money, buy birds that will give you the results that you want, with certainty, in one or two generations. But doing it the long way is fun, and such thrills come from opening the nest box to a clutch of chicks in colors you never expected.

To discover the true background of your parent birds, you would have to breed their babies with one another, or breed parent to offspring. Inbreeding is sometimes done by breeders to purify color or enhance a color, but this practice is not recommended for the hobbyist and can result in severely crippled and ill-fated birds that may pass on "bad" genes to future generations.

It may be difficult to find a bird with "pure" genes or a bird whose genes have not been mixed with many colors. You really never know what you're going to get unless you stick with a pair and their subsequent generations through a few years of breeding. If you enter into this endeavor with the idea of having fun with it, and appreciating every baby you produce regardless of color, you're on the right track. No lovebird color is superior to another, but there seem to be breeder favorites, some colors that are more sought after than others. When a color is very new it becomes popular and the birds are very expensive as a result. It only takes three or four years for the price on these "new" birds to go down, so you can get one for a fairly inexpensive price if you're patient.

This is just an overview of lovebird color mutations; there's certainly more to learn. It can be a confusing and complicated science, though the lovebirds seem to know what they're doing. Becoming good at predicting the colors of your lovebird's offspring comes more from practice than research. It gets easier every year to look at your bird's offspring and know from experience, without the technical jargon, which birds should be paired together for the best looking babies or for a particular color. Pairing the "right" parents is something you easily get the hang of with a few years of trial and error and close record-keeping.

Here's a fun tip: You will be able to tell the basic mutations of your babies when they are only a day old. The chicks with the orange fluff on their backs are in the green mutation group and the chicks with the white fluffy down are in the blue mutation group. You can also tell something about the chicks by the color of their eyes, whether they are red or black—red can indicate a lutino, creamino, or a clear-eyed mutation.

If you want to learn more about lovebird genetics, there are clubs and societies all over the country dedicated to lovebirds that will be happy to help you. There are even peach-faced lovebird genetic calculators on the Internet that will determine what offspring will occur from a certain pairing simply by entering in the information.

SHOWING Your Lovebird

P art of the fun of breeding and keeping lovebirds is showing them. At a show you get to meet other lovebird enthusiasts and learn about how other breeders find success in the nest box. A lovebird show is a place to see birds in a wide array of mutations and to see some of the rare species that you wouldn't normally find in a pet shop.

WHY SHOW YOUR LOVEBIRD?

People show their lovebirds for fun and to develop a name in the bird community. A breeder with many winning lovebirds is likely to fetch a high price for her babies. A bird show is a place to buy and trade lovebirds and to learn about the hobby. At a show you will find friends and mentors. Everyone at the show is as passionate about lovebirds as you are, and most people are willing to share their knowledge with a newcomer to the hobby. There's always a risk in transporting your birds and in allowing them to come in contact with other birds, but realize that everyone is in the same situation, and that most people are conscientious about bringing only healthy birds to a show.

THE SHOW CAGE

Most birds are shown in small cages known as show cages, which are designed to accentuate the color and size of the bird. A show cage has bars only on the front panel, with the back and sides painted a very light blue or white. The show cage is light and easy for the show steward (the person who moves the birds around on the show bench) to move around. You can show in another type of cage, but you will be putting your bird at a disadvantage. You can purchase a show cage through ads in bird magazines.

When you're showing your bird, you should not use litter in the show cage that will make your bird look dirty, such as newspaper (the ink can rub off onto the feathers). Litter that's not very absorbent can allow fecal material to stick to your bird. Some people use crushed corn, chicken feed, or rabbit pellets as litter. Give your bird some seed and attach a small, tube-type waterer to provide water, but be sure that it doesn't spill. An accident can spoil the look of your bird's feathers.

What Happens at a Show?

Most bird shows begin early in the morning with bird check-in and a veterinarian looking over the contestants. Lovebirds are entered into a color classification, so the green peach-faced are judged against other green peach-faced. The winner of this class goes on to compete against the other birds that have won their classes, and the winner of the division, in this cases, the peach-faced division, goes on to compete against the winners of the other divisions for the Best in Show title. If it's a lovebird show, only lovebirds will compete for the Best in Show title. If it's an all-bird show, the best lovebird will compete against other species in the final round of judging.

When you check your lovebird into the show, make sure that it's going to be judged in the proper class. Ask someone to look at your bird if you're uncertain of its color. If you're new at showing, you can enter the "novice" division, and birds with clipped wings can also be entered this division. In most shows, any bird entered must be wearing a closed band for identification purposes, so only bring banded birds to the show.

Once your bird is checked in, you will get a show schedule that will indicate when your bird is going to be shown. While you are watching your bird on the judge's bench, try not to indicate which bird is yours; this is considered rude and can get your bird disqualified. If your bird is a beloved pet, it may see you and do a frantic dance to get to you, so stay out of sight if you can. Once the judge has chosen the top three birds on the bench, he or she will give an explanation of why those birds were chosen. This is a real learning moment, so be sure to listen. You can occasionally approach a judge after the show is over and ask him or her to explain to you why your bird wasn't chosen, if that's the case. Use this opportunity to learn, not to be defensive or challenging. There will be other shows.

The winners in their class, division, and show, as well as the best novice bird, will all receive a ribbon, and sometimes even a trophy or cup. But don't be discouraged if you don't win anything; showing is for the fun of the hobby. Your birds are still wonderful pets, even if they don't have a ribbon hanging on their cages.

The Lovebird Standard

It may seem that the lovebirds at a show are being judged against each other, but they are really being judged against a standard, an

At bird shows, lovebirds are entered into a color classification. Make sure your bird is judged in the correct category. These birds are a normal peach-faced and a white-faced blue.

All lovebirds are judged according to the standard. This masked lovebird would be judged against other masked lovebirds.

ideal lovebird whose qualities the judges look for in the lovebirds being shown. The lovebird show standard includes the following criteria:

Conformation

Beak: neat and well tucked in; head full and round; eyes centered, clear and bright. *Neck:* full and wide. *Shoulders:* no appearance of the neckline. *Breast:* deep, broad, and well rounded, tapering gradually to the tail. *Back line:* not slack or hollow; almost straight. *Wings:* held neatly in line with the body; flights must not droop or cross. *Tail:* held neatly in line with body. *Legs and feet:* straight and strong, firmly gripping the perch.

Size, color, deportment (posture and manner) and condition of the bird are also important factors. The scale of points for the peach-faced lovebird is as follows:

Size	15
Conformation	45
Head	15
Body	15
Wings and Tail	10
Feet	5
Color	15
Condition	15
Deportment	10

CONDITIONING AND TRAINING A LOVEBIRD FOR SHOWING

You should only take a lovebird to a show when it is in perfect condition and when it has been trained to know what to expect from a show. Never take a lovebird to a show when it is ill, molting, nesting, or has never been in a show cage.

If you plan on showing your lovebird, purchase a show-quality bird from a reputable breeder.

The first thing to do to find out if a lovebird is suitable for showing is to compare it to the lovebird standard. If you feel that the bird is close to the standard, that it's large and healthy looking, it might be a good candidate. You can supplement a bird's diet with items that are good for the condition of the feathers, such as hardboiled egg and a little olive oil on the seed, but go light on the oil. About six weeks to a month before the show, you can pull any feathers that are broken or otherwise damaged. Be conservative about pulling feathers, however, as this can lead to bleeding. Three weeks before the show, begin misting your bird every day to encourage preening. Three days before the show you can add a few drops of glycerin to the water to provide a shine.

A few weeks before the show, begin show training your lovebird by placing it inside the show cage. Do this for a few minutes a day, extending the amount of time the bird spends in the cage. The show judge will use a "wand" to move your lovebird around the cage. You should train your bird to accept this by using a chopstick to make your bird turn around or hop perch to perch. Your bird should neither attack the stick nor be terrified of it.

A few days before the show, have a friend come over and perform a "mock" show, just as it would happen in the real show. Have your friend be the judge and take your birds in their show cages to a new area that they're not used to. Invite an audience if you want, and play some music and the television to provide the commotion that your birds will experience at the show. If your birds handle this mock show with poise, they are ready for the big time! You can find out about bird shows from your local bird club, or by contacting the African Lovebird Society.

APPENDIX Harmful and Safe Plants

Houseplants are a serious temptation for lovebirds, which are naturally attracted to them. Even one nibble of a toxic plant can poison your lovebird and cause death. The following is a partial list of toxic and safe houseplants.

Partial List of Harmful Indoor Plants

Amaryllis—bulbs
American Yew
Avocado, Azalea—leaves
Balsam Pear—seeds, outer rind of fruit
Baneberry—berries, root
Bird of Paradise—seeds
Black Locust
Blue-green Algae—some forms toxic
Boxwood—leaves, stems
Buckthorn—fruit, bark
Buttercup—sap, bulbs
Caladium—leaves
Calla Lily—leaves
Castor Bean—also castor oil, leaves
Chalice Vine/Trumpet vine
Christmas Candle—sap
Clematis/Virginia, Bower, Coral Plant—seeds
Cowslip/Marsh Marigold, Daffodil—bulbs
Daphne—berries
Datura—berries
Deadly Amanita
Death Camas
Delphinium
Deffenbachia/Dumb Cane—leaves
Eggplant—fruit okay
Elephants Ear/Taro—leaves, stem
English Ivy berries, leaves
English Yew
False Henbane
Fly Agaric Mushroom—Deadly Amanita
Foxglove—leaves, seeds
Golden Chain/Laburnum
Hemlock

Henbane—seeds
Holly—berries
Horse Chestnut/Buckeye—nuts, twigs
Hyacinth—bulbs
Hydrangea—flower bud
Indian Turnip/Jack-in-Pulpit
Iris/Blue Flag—bulbs
Jack-in-the-Pulpit
Japanese Yew—needles, seeds
Java Bean—uncooked
Juniper—needles, stems, berries
Lantana—immature berries
Larkspur
Laurel
Lily of the Valley
Lobelia
Locoweed
Lords and Ladies/Cuckoopint
Marijuana/Hemp—leaves
Mayapple—fruit is safe
Mescal Beans—seeds
Mistletoe—berries
Mock Orange—fruit
Monkshood—leaves, root
Morning Glory
Narcissus—bulbs
Nightshade—all varieties
Oleander
Philodendron—leaves and stem
Poinsettia
Poison Ivy—sap
Poison Oak—sap

Pokeweed/Inkberry
Potato—eyes, new shoots
Privet
Rhododendron
Rhubarb—leaves
Rosary Peas/Indian Licorice
Skunk Cabbage
Snowdrop

Snow on the Mountain
Sweet Pea—seeds, fruit
Tobacco—leaves
Virginia Creeper—sap
Water Hemlock
Western Yew
Wisteria
Yam bean

Partial List of Safe Houseplants

Acacia Aloe
African Violet
Baby's Tears
Bamboo
Begonia
Bougainvillea
Chickweed
Christmas Cactus
Cissus/Kangaroo Vine
Coffee
Coleus
Corn Plant
Crabapple
Dandelion
Dogwood
Donkey Tail
Dracena Varieties
Ferns
Figs
Gardenia
Grape Ivy
Hens and Chickens

Herbs
Jade Plant
Kalanchoe
Marigold
Monkey Plant
Mother-in-Law's Tongue
Nasturtium
Natal Plum
Pepperomia
Petunia
Pittosporum
Prayer Plant
Nettle
Purple Passion/Velvet
Schefflera (Umbrella)
Sensitive Plant
Spider Plant
Swedish Ivy
Thistle
Wandering Jew
White Clover
Zebra Plant

RESOURCES

African Lovebird Society
PO Box 142
San Marcos, CA 92079-0142
Website: www.africanlovebirdsociety.com

The African Lovebird Society is an international organization dedicated to the keeping, breeding, and showing of the nine species of lovebirds. The society publishes the journal *Agapornis World*, which each member receives as part of membership.

AFA Watchbird
American Federation of Aviculture, Inc.
PO Box 7312
N. Kansas City, MO 64116
Phone: (816) 421-BIRD
Fax: (816) 421-3214
Website: www.afa.birds.org

The AFA is a nonprofit organization dedicated to the promotion of aviculture and the conservation of avian wildlife through the encouragement of captive-breeding programs, scientific research, and the education of the general public. The AFA publishes a bi-monthly magazine called *AFA Watchbird*.

Association of Avian Veterinarians
PO Box 811720
Boca Raton, FL 33481
Phone: (561) 393-8901
Fax: (561) 393-8902
Website: www.aav.org
Email: AAVCTRLOFC@aol.com

AAV membership is comprised of veterinarians from private practice, zoos, universities and industry, veterinary educators, researchers and technicians, and veterinary students. Serves as a resource for bird owners who are looking for certified avian veterinarians.

Bird Talk Magazine
Subscription Dept.
3 Burroughs
Irvine, CA 92618
Phone: (949) 855-8822
Fax: (949) 855-3045
Website: www.animalnetwork.com

Bird Talk is a monthly magazine noted for its directory of avian breeders, as well as its informative articles and columns on health care, conservation, and behavior.

Bird Times
Pet Publishing, Inc.
7-L Dundas Circle
Greensboro, NC 27407
Phone: (336) 292-4047
Fax: (336) 292-4272
Website: www.birdtimes.com
Email: info@petpublishing.com

Bird Times is a source of entertaining and authoritative information about birds. Articles include bird breed profiles, medical reports, training advice, bird puzzles, and stories about special birds.

The Gabriel Foundation
PO Box 11477
Aspen, CO 81612
Phone: (970) 963-2620
Toll-free: (877) 923-1009
Fax: (970) 963-2218
Website: www.thegabrielfoundation.org
Email: Gabriel@thegabrielfoundation.org

The Gabriel Foundation is a nonprofit organization dedicated to promoting education, rescue, adoption, and sanctuary for parrots.

Midwest Avian Research Expo (MARE)
10430 Dewhurst Road
Elyria, OH 44036
Website: www.mare-expo.org

MARE is a nonprofit group dedicated to education and fundraising for avian research projects.

National Animal Poison Control Center/ASPCA
(888) 426-4435
(900) 680-0000

In a life-and-death poisoning situation you can call this hotline for 24-hour emergency information. There is a charge for this service.

INDEX

Photo Credits:

Herbert Axelrod: 12, 33, 152
Joan Balzarini: 21, 79, 108, 126, 131
Delia Berlin: 56
Isabelle Francais: 38, 47, 48, 50, 73, 88, 130
Michael Gilroy: 22, 25, 34, 43, 65, 91, 120, 127, 133, 151
Erik Ilasenko: 19, 35, 41, 53, 62, 64, 67, 71, 93, 95, 122, 125, 145
Bonnie Jay: 27, 28, 57, 68, 72, 117, 134, 143
H. Mayer: 70, 82, 102, 121, 141, 153
Horst Muller: 16
Robert Pearcy: 23, 44, 136
H. Reinhard: 11
Vince Serbin: 112, 116, 137
Lara Stern: 115
Karen Taylor: 97
John Tyson: 9, 30, 51, 60, 74, 85, 99, 101, 103, 105, 106, 109, 111, 138, 139
Louise van der Meid: 76, 83, 123
Vogelpark Walstrode: 13, 17
M. Vriends: 15, 37, 39